SAFETY CAPACITY

LEADERSHIP PRACTICES FOR FAILING SAFELY

By Martha L. Acosta, EdD

First Edition

Pre-accident Investigation Media
Santa Fe, New Mexico, USA

Copyright © 2024 by Martha L. Acosta

All rights reserved. No part of this book may be reproduced, stored in a retrieval system, or transmitted in any form, by any means, including electronic, photocopying, recording, or otherwise, without prior written permission of the author. This book may not be translated and published in translation without prior written permission of the author.

Martha L. Acosta
PO Box 8501
Santa Fe, NM 87504-8501
USA

Library of Congress Cataloging-in-Publication Data: 2023911085

This book is dedicated to a dear friend, a committed mentor, a steadfast champion, a great neighbor, a fellow culinary and travel adventurer, and an inspirational e-bike gang leader. I am so grateful for you.

FOREWORD

When my colleague and friend Martha Acosta asked me if I would consider writing the foreword to this book, I agreed immediately. You see, when you write a forward, you get the privilege of reading the book a little bit before its formal release—which is a sort of like getting a taste of the delicious batter before the cookies have finished baking. I knew I'd love it because Martha and I have a shared history working with the new safety paradigm she outlines here. We both were involved with the Human and Organizational Performance (HOP) approach to industrial safety very early in its origins, which was an incredibly exciting time for both of us. I also knew the book would be accessible, quick-witted, and astute, and that I would certainly learn something new from it about how leaders can shape the organizational systems that make for productive and safe work. This book will change how you lead by refocusing your attention on what matters most, ensuring that when a failure happens, it happens safely.

In my talks to business and safety leaders around the world, I often play the video of a fateful day in the life of alligator wrestler Kenny Cypress, who was nearly killed when a drop of his sweat landed deep in the mouth of the alligator he was wrestling. This triggered the alligator to bite down on Kenny's head. Kenny survived, with the help of onlookers who together managed to pry the mouth of the gator back open. But Kenny's misadventure illustrates the point that, as hazardous as it is to wrestle alligators, the most stable and predictable part of Kenny's work was the alligator itself. Alligators are biologically designed to bite down hard when something hits the inside of their mouths, and thus the real hazard, the safety wild card, was not the gator, but the organizational system that Kenny was working within that had no built-in capacity to fail safely.

If you do a high-risk operation and nothing bad happens, I bet you can't tell me if you were good or if you were lucky. Kenny was lucky—there were enough people nearby who together were able to loosen the gator's bite, but that wasn't by design, it was simply luck. I would argue that your facilities have all the components needed to have to have a catastrophic failure right now. You don't have to add anything when you have electricity, high pressure, chemicals, heavy equipment, heights, and all those things that come together in a way that gets companies like yours on the news. When you put a worker in such a facility and give them a job where the only defense they have against getting hurt or killed is that they'll do the job perfectly, you are making your very own alligator wrestling show.

I play the Kenny video to shift how leaders like you see safety. To counter the notion that workers are in charge of safety, and that without their mistakes there would be no accidents. To get leaders like you curious about the ways things can and will go wrong, because perfect humans, perfect equipment, and prefect procedures don't exist. To help leaders stop seeing safety as an outcome and to start seeing it as a capacity. The truth is that leaders like you don't manage accidents (unintentional deviations from the expected) you manage your company's ability to have accidents safely and to have failures without consequence.

This book will help you do that. Martha's book is a practical guide for integrating the principles of HOP into your leadership practice, and to build safety capacity into your organizational, operational, and psychological systems. The main message of this book—the big write-it-down and take-it-home message—is remarkably important: leaders must deliberately build their organization's capacity for safety.

I hope you enjoy this book, that you find it incredibly useful, and that you as learn much from it as I did. You are in for a treat.

Todd Conklin, PhD
Santa Fe, New Mexico

CONTENTS

DEDICATION 5

FOREWORD 7

CONTENTS 11

FIGURES 14

INTRODUCTION 15

CHAPTER 1: WHAT IS SAFETY CAPACITY? 19

    Failure is the occurrence of the unexpected, unintended, or unwanted 22

    Leaders must build safety capacity to do dangerous work 23

    Organizational Capacity 26

    Operational Capacity 27

    Psychological Capacity 28

    Creating safety capacity in a crisis 30

    Safety Capacity Reflection Questions 34

CHAPTER 2: SHAPE A SHARED PURPOSE 37

    Is your organization purpose driven or ego driven? 40

    Purpose brings diverse roles and perspectives together and helps workers make better decisions 42

Can you articulate your team's shared purpose? ... 43
How does a shared purpose build safety capacity? ... 45
Identify and communicate shared purpose as part of your regular leadership practice ... 46
Shared Purpose Reflection Questions ... 47

CHAPTER 3: CULTIVATE NETWORKS OF RELATIONSHIPS ... **49**

Organizations are systems of meaning ... 52
Improve the quality of your relationships ... 54
Broaden and diversify your relationships ... 56
Secure sponsorship and mentorship for you and your team ... 58
How do relationships build safety capacity? ... 60
Cultivate networks of relationships as part of your regular leadership practice ... 61
Relationship Networks Reflection Questions ... 64

CHAPTER 4: FOSTER OPENNESS AND CURIOSITY ... **65**

Errors are normal ... 67
Certainty is the enemy of learning ... 69
Safety has been relying on "no, don't" instead of "yes, and" for too long ... 70
Encourage inquiry over advocacy ... 71
Set learning goals aligned with performance goals ... 73
Disrupt the learning curve ... 74
How do openness and curiosity create safety capacity? ... 76
Foster openness and curiosity as part of a regular leadership practice ... 77
Openness and Curiosity Reflection Questions ... 79

CHAPTER 5: DRIVE CRITICAL THINKING 81

Continually reassess assumptions and presumed
outcomes in the face of change 83

Address power dynamics and create
psychological safety 85

Stop solution-finding and start problem-solving 88

How does critical thinking create safety capacity? 90

Build critical thinking into your regular
leadership practice 91

Critical Thinking Reflection Questions 95

CHAPTER 6: EXPERIMENT 97

Experimentation is simply a learning technique for
increasing certainty 99

An experiment begins with a hypothesis 102

An experiment is limited and controlled 103

In an experiment, failure is expected and mitigated 104

How does experimentation create safety capacity? 105

Integrate experimentation into your regular
leadership practice 106

Experimentation Reflection Questions 110

CHAPTER 7: DEVELOP EMOTIONAL RESILIENCY 113

Emotions play a fundamental role in all social systems 116

Awareness and acceptance of emotions 117

Empathy underlies trust, facilitates collaboration,
and improves problem-solving 119

How does emotional resiliency create safety capacity? 121

Emotional resiliency is an essential daily leadership practice 122

Emotional Resiliency Reflection Questions 129

CHAPTER 8: BUILD SAFETY CAPACITY 131

Leadership is an important safety system that influences all levels of the organization 133

Shape a shared purpose 133

Cultivate networks of relationships 134

Foster openness and curiosity 135

Drive critical thinking 135

Experiment 136

Develop emotional resiliency 136

ABOUT THE AUTHOR 139

FIGURES

Figure 1: Safety Capacity Model 24

Figure 2: Relationship Network Map 63

Figure 3: Critical Thinking Process 94

Figure 4: VUCA Johari Window 100

Figure 5: Basic Feelings 122

Figure 6: Emotional Agility Process 124

INTRODUCTION

Safety enables courage. In high school, a college counselor asked me what I wanted out of life. I described the passage in the Odyssey when Odysseus asks his men to tie him to the mast and cover their ears so he can hear the siren song without them driving the ship into the rocks. This exchange has stayed with me over the years because it reminds me of what safety leaders do: they enable adventurous, driven, and curious people to surpass limitations and achieve ambitious goals. Safety leaders allow scientists to work with hazardous materials and discover their mysteries. They devise ways in which first responders can go headlong into a disaster and save lives. They create the conditions for engineers to erect marvels of human ingenuity and for physicians and biochemists to achieve medical miracles.

This book is for safety leaders. You don't have to be a manager or formally supervise a team to be a leader. *Leaders are those who enable others to contribute fully to a shared purpose and fulfill their individual and collective goals.* Whether you are a director of environment, safety, and health; an industrial hygienist; an on-the-job training specialist; or an executive of a company whose work is subject to government regulation, you are a safety leader. You create the capacity for safety in your organization. It doesn't matter if you have just now realized, while reading this introduction, that you are a leader. Nor does it matter if you have understood yourself to be a leader for decades. The leadership practices I examine in this book are fundamental to enabling others to be exceptional—safely.

In the chapters that follow, I first explain, through the lens of organizational learning and development, what safety capacity is. Safety capacity allows you and your organization to foster a more constructive relationship to failure, with failure defined as simply the occurrence of the unexpected, unintended, or unwanted. My conceptualization of safety capacity is based on the work and research of those who built the foundations of Human Performance, Safety-II, and Human and Organizational Performance (HOP). I have had the privilege of participating in this shift in safety thinking since my early days implementing Human Performance Improvement at Los Alamos National Laboratory. My current contribution to this thinking is organizing safety capacity into three areas that leaders can influence, helping leaders like you to direct their efforts based on their role in the organization. It's important to me that this book provides you with a blueprint for directing your leadership to build capacity and—perhaps most importantly—helps you to recognize that your leadership, no matter where it occupies the organizational chart, is critical to the safe execution of hazardous operations.

The focus of this book is to detail six leadership practices that build an organization's capacity to fail safely and therefore be safe. I draw on the scholarship of members of the Academy of Management and professors at Harvard and other well-respected business schools with whom I have had the honor to work and learn. My objective in this book is to translate this knowledge from corporate head offices and elite leadership programs to the field, factory floor, laboratory, emergency room, and demolition or construction site. These leadership practices may seem obvious, but in my decades of developing leaders, I have not found them to be commonly practiced. Although the evidence supports just how important they are, they take conscious intent and continuous commitment. These practices are (1) identifying and communicating a shared purpose; (2) cultivating a network of meaningful relationships; (3) fostering openness and curiosity; (4) driving critical thinking; (5) experimenting; and (6) developing the emotional resilience to be vulnerable. If this list raises uncomfortable feelings yet you intuitively know these things are important, this book is for you. Even if you are skeptical that these practices will make a difference to safety, this book will provide supporting research and include numerous examples to help you find value in the following pages. I sincerely hope this will be a useful guide in your leadership and safety journeys.

CHAPTER 1: WHAT IS SAFETY CAPACITY?

With nine years of documented and unresolved O-ring leakage and erosion, and 82% of launches having photographic evidence of foam loss and/or impact, were the space shuttle disasters a result of mounting failures or an unwillingness to examine them?

Failure is inevitable—disastrous consequences are not. O-ring erosion was a well-known and alarming failure to Thiokol engineers working on the solid booster rockets used in space shuttle launches.[1] Yet these failures had not compromised a mission in nine years—until the space shuttle *Challenger* exploded upon launch on January 28, 1986, killing its crew. Foam strikes were another regular and frequent failure during space shuttle launches, sometimes causing significant damage, but more often not. Despite photographic evidence of foam loss for a vast majority of launches, this failure was largely dismissed—right up until it resulted in the loss of seven lives aboard the space shuttle *Columbia* on February 1, 2003.[2] One member of the Roger Commission investigating the *Challenger* event called the agency's practice of ignoring failures without a bad outcome "a kind of Russian roulette."

Why do the space shuttle disasters come to mind so readily when discussing safety? Because we witnessed the tragedies as they happened—some of us watched it on televisions wheeled into our classrooms or when crowded around the television in the living room with our families. But what we witnessed wasn't failure—it was the disastrous outcome of many failures, some directly causal, others indirect, some barely consequential. When we watched the successful launch of the *Columbia* just two weeks before the catastrophic launch of the *Challenger*, we witnessed the uneventful outcome of many of the same failures that would lead to tragedy 17 years later. Yes, *the same failures* with a different outcome due to the specific constellation of conditions and tolerances of that particular launch.

---

[1] Oscar Hauptman and Genji Iwaki, *The Final Voyage of the Challenger* (Boston: Harvard Business School, 1991), https://hbsp.harvard.edu/product/691039-PDF-ENG.

[2] Richard M. Bohmer, Amy C. Edmondson, and Michael A. Roberto, *Columbia's Final Mission*, (Boston: Harvard Business School, 2004), https://www.hbs.edu/faculty/Pages/item.aspx?num=31131.

Failure is the occurrence of the unexpected, unintended, or unwanted

When your hypothesis is not supported by evidence, when something meant to hold together falls apart, when a situation or object turns out to be different from what you thought it was—these are examples of failure. Failure need not have a bad outcome. As romantic comedies teach us, mistaken identities, wrong turns, and shattered expectations can result in happily ever after. Unfortunately, failures without immediate or sizeable consequences tend to be ignored. Without a change in mindset, we only notice failure when it hurts.

Confusing failure with bad outcomes promotes a *fear of failure* that discourages us from being curious about what we might learn from having things go wrong. If we recognize that failure doesn't have to lead to a disastrous outcome (in fact, it rarely does), it becomes easier to see the failures that are all around us. This awareness of everyday failure is important because if we don't recognize inconsequential failure, we can't appreciate the importance of our capacity to withstand and respond constructively to failure.

How long can you hold your breath? Being able to hold one's breath is critically important to personal safety when swimming. It's a capacity that we either build, through breathing exercises, for example, or destroy, by, for example, smoking. Certain conditions, like the temperature of the water, might reduce your capacity to hold your breath, so your tolerance for failure while swimming will be lower on a chilly day. Swimming is a calculated risk. You wouldn't put your child in the water without assurances that there was the capacity to withstand the consequences of failure, such as the presence of a lifeguard, the availability of flotation devices, and the child's ability to hold their breath. Work is also a calculated risk with many opportunities to fail. Organizations that must do work safely to operate—in other words, those that do dangerous work—build the capacity for failure into their organizations, operations, and people. For example, my municipal pool hires lifeguards (an organizational capacity to respond to failure), provides a variety of floaties (an operational capacity to mitigate a hazard), and offers free water confidence classes to help people overcome their fear of swimming (a psychological capacity).

Leaders must build safety capacity to do dangerous work

Safety capacity is the extent to which organizations, their operations, and their people can absorb the destructive and constructive consequences of failure. I use the word absorb in two senses: the first is like a thick safety mat that absorbs and disperses the energy of a fall, and the second is like a curious child absorbing learning like a sponge and adapting quickly to new challenges. Safety capacity

> **Safety capacity is the extent to which organizations can absorb the consequences of failure.**

not only allows organizations to avoid catastrophe, but it also helps them to learn, innovate, and thrive. Safety capacity is built at three levels: the first is *organizational capacity*: how well the organization upholds safety when responding to strategic pressure, and how well it addresses systemic organizational weaknesses that could impact safety. Strategic pressures are challenges that arise from competitive forces, supply chain issues, needs of customers or other stakeholders, and regulatory, political, environmental, and other external forces. Organizational weaknesses can result from systemic management issues such as financial strain or mismanagement, ineffective internal business practices, poor communication channels, inadequate leadership, and inability to learn and improve.

The second level is *operational capacity*, which is how well the organization identifies inherent and emergent hazards and error-prone conditions in operations and creates barriers and controls against them. Examples of inherent hazards are radiation when working with nuclear materials, or gravity when working at height. Emergent hazards arise when conditions vary, such as working with electricity in inclement weather. Error-prone conditions are those that push the limits of human and engineered tolerances, such as a cockpit with too many gages or heavy machinery working on soft, unstable ground.

The third level of capacity, which allows for the creation of capacity organizationally and operationally, is *psychological capacity*: the extent to which culture, leadership, and mindset allow for candid conversation, expression of differences, experimentation, vulnerability, curiosity, and dissent. In other words, psychological capacity is the extent to which the culture of the organization tolerates being uncomfortable in service of learning.

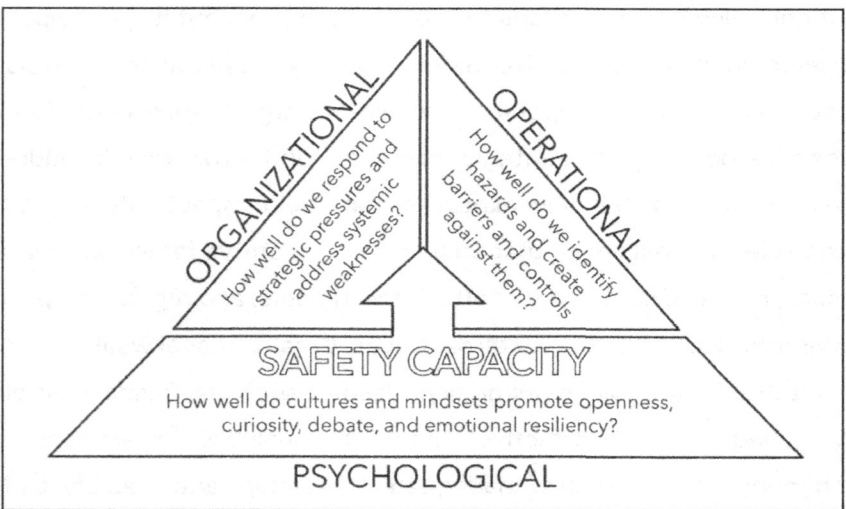

Figure 1: Safety Capacity Model

To explain safety capacity, let's examine two disasters, only one of which resulted in tragedy. On January 16, 2003, the space shuttle *Columbia* launched for the final time. Less than a minute and a half into the launch, foam shed from the external tank of the rocket launcher and hit the left wing of the manned orbiter. Despite this, the orbiter successfully made it into space and would not return to Earth for 16 days. On August 5, 2010, 700,000 tons of rock collapsed in Chile's San José Mine, burying 33 miners more than 700 meters below ground.[3] Seventeen days later, with all miners alive but sick and starving, rescuers were able to reach the miners to provide communication and supplies. Both the *Columbia* and the San José Mine disasters had inherent safety capacity—the ability to withstand or avoid dire consequences for a period of time, allowing a window of recovery. It would be 16 days before the *Columbia*'s wing would be tested by the stress of entry into Earth's atmosphere, but the orbiter could have stayed in space longer. It was 17 days before the miners would get fresh water, food, and medicine, but they may have survived a few more days. In the 16-day window of recovery, NASA did not assess or control the hazard created by the foam-shedding event, and the seven-person crew of the *Columbia* died. In its 17-day window of recovery (even while not knowing if the miners were dead or alive), the Chilean government's rescue team innovated technology to reach the mine's safety refuge and saved 33 lives. Are mining engineers just smarter than aerospace engineers? Probably not. Was Chile's mining industry better at safety than the American aerospace industry? Absolutely not. Did the San José Mine have better organizational, operational, and psychological capacity than the Space Shuttle Program? No, no, and no. In fact, comparing the disasters,

---

3   Amy C. Edmondson, Faaiza Rashid, and Herman B. Leonard, *The 2010 Chilean Mining Rescue*, (A) (Boston: Harvard Business School, 2012), https://www.hbs.edu/faculty/Pages/item.aspx?num=41081.

both the mine and the program suffered from significant deficiencies in all three safety capacities.

Organizational Capacity

Both the Space Shuttle Program and the San José mine sacrificed safety under strategic pressures and failed to address their organizational weaknesses. Both organizations operated under tremendous production pressure. The promise that NASA made to the White House and Congress when securing funding for the Shuttle Program was to make space flight as routine as flying a 747. This unrealistic expectation, compounded with competition from the European Space Agency, incentivized NASA to commit to launching at a rate of 50 commercial and scientific missions per year. But within 30 years, only 135 missions were flown. In contrast, the San José Mine made good on its potential—yet this potential incentivized a similar risk. The mine had been operational since 1889. At the time of its collapse in 2010, it was still producing $22,000 of copper every day. The mine also held gold deposits estimated to be in the billions of dollars. As one of the few privately owned mines in Chile—and with continued seismic activity in the region—the operators of the mine were racing to get the most out of it while they still could.

These strategic pressures created organizational weaknesses that were not addressed. NASA's political challenges left it grappling with budget cuts, interagency red tape, and increasing time and cost pressures imposed on suppliers. The risks and uncertainties of its operations were downplayed and minimized by leaders who provided hollow assurances to Congress and commercial clients. Politics also affected the San José Mine. Chile's complicated history of political upheaval left the San José Mine largely without regulation. Like a teenager without supervision, the mining operator engaged in disorganized dynamiting, drilling, and extraction. This produced 16 kilometers of mostly unmapped and poorly supported tunnels. In short, organizational issues proved detrimental to safe operations in both cases.

Operational Capacity

Both the Space Shuttle Program and the San José Mine did not have the operational capacity required to adequately respond to inherent and emerging hazards and error-prone conditions. Immediately after the launch of the *Columbia*, engineers reviewed video showing an alarming volume of foam loss and determined that foam had hit the wing of the orbiter. However, the video quality was not sufficient to determine damage. The camera lenses had been poorly maintained because budget cuts had reduced camera staff. Attempts to get additional imagery from other agencies failed because proper interagency communication channels were unclear. Attempts to classify the foam strike as a risk to safety of flight, which would have spurred action, failed because the Debris Assessment Team did not report to the Mission Management Team, resulting in no direct communication between them. Schedule pressures, and fears that *unvetted* problems would make it to the press influenced mission managers to downplay and ultimately dismiss the concerns of engineers.

The San José Mine's inability to control hazards in its operation was more obvious, and likewise arose from organizational issues—more accurately an absence of organization. When the mine collapsed, there were no escape ladders in the ventilation shafts, no back-up exits. There was a 50-square-meter safety refuge where miners could shelter in an emergency, but it was not adequately stocked with food, water, or medical supplies. When the 33 miners made it there, they found expired medicine, two canisters of oxygen, and only enough food and liquids to keep 10 miners alive for two days.

Psychological Capacity

To overcome and correct the organizational and operational deficiencies they faced, the engineers at NASA and the miners in the San José Mine would need exceptional psychological (interpersonal, emotional, and cognitive) resources. Unfortunately, both the Space Shuttle Program and the San José Mine fostered cultures, leadership behaviors, and worker mindsets that undermined *psychological safety*, defined as "a shared belief that it is safe to take interpersonal risks." Former shuttle astronaut Jim Bagian told federal investigators, "At senior levels, during the 1990s, dissent was not tolerated, and therefore people learned if you wanted to survive in the organization, you had to keep your mouth shut."[4] When the Mission Management Team of the *Columbia* flight decided in a meeting that the foam strike was not going to be acted upon, engineers in the room were distressed and angry, but no one could overcome their fear of speaking up. One senior engineer mustered the courage to write an email to Mission Management detailing the false assumptions and risks of their decision, but his coworkers urged him not to jeopardize his career by sending it. He didn't.

The San José Mine fostered a different, but just as psychologically unsafe, culture of masculine bravado. Because the San José Mine was both highly productive and extremely unsafe, its miners were paid 30 percent more

---

4 Richard M. Bohmer, Amy C. Edmondson, and Michael A. Roberto, *Columbia's Final Mission*, (Boston: Harvard Business School, 2004), https://www.hbs.edu/faculty/Pages/item.aspx?num=31131.

than the competitive wage. This wage was so attractive it drew a local sports celebrity, who later became one of the trapped miners. The higher wage fostered an *elite miner* mindset, where dodging falling rocks and avoiding debris slides were considered requisite athletic skills (and an opportunity to demonstrate masculine prowess), so barriers and controls were not created. The miners' response to the death of a geologist in 2007 illustrates their culture and mindset: this fatal incident in the mine prompted a shutdown and an angry reaction from miners. They expressed frustration at "being punished" for the actions of an inexperienced outsider who couldn't handle the conditions. As the problem was perceived as a deficiency in the geologist, safety did not improve after the incident.

When failure occurred in both cases—foam striking the wing of the Space Shuttle *Columbia*, and the entrance to the San José Mine in Chile collapsing—the operations of both organizations were in an equally sorry state of diminished safety capacity. However, when the capacity to save lives started ticking away, one operation was unable to do so, while the other succeeded in almost the same amount of time. In truth, neither NASA nor the operator of the San José Mine did anything to recover after their respective failures. NASA never assessed the damage to the orbiter's wing. It never attempted to fix the damage before calling the ship back into the Earth's atmosphere. And the operator of the San José Mine? They called in rescue personnel, who attempted to reach the miners through existing ventilation shafts but determined it was unsafe to do so. Then they walked away.

The miners were not saved because the mining company mustered what was needed to overcome the poor safety conditions it had created. What saved them was the almost spontaneous emergence of a new organization brimming with safety capacity that its self-appointed leaders created. At the time of the collapse, the Chilean president, Sebastián Piñera, was traveling with the minister of mining, Laurence Golborne. They knew San José was a private mine and not part of Codelco, the government-run National Copper Corporation of Chile. They also knew that, although it was customary for the mining operator to take responsibility for a safety incident, the owner and operator of the San José Mine was unable to save the miners. The president decided on the spot that the Ministry of Mining would take charge. When Minister Golborne arrived on the scene on August 7, he found the owners of the mine in shock and the families of the miners in a state of panic. What he didn't find was trust, information, or leadership—so he created it.

Creating safety capacity in a crisis

A *shared purpose* to find the miners—dead or alive—was the catalyst for an emerging organization of rescuers. The rescue team self-assembled from a shared sense of duty and humanity. Experts and leaders from the Chilean and international mining community just showed up to help, bringing workers, machinery, and vehicles. At first, they found no one in charge, but once President Piñera took responsibility, Codelco selected André Sougarret to lead the rescue. The first thing Sougarret had to do was stop all the people who had assembled to haphazardly drill and pickaxe the site in search of the miners. He developed a strategy that was communicated daily to the press, family, volunteers, and experts at the mine. The strategy had one clear purpose that was reiterated every day: find the miners, dead or alive. To that end, he cleared a drilling perimeter where only technical teams could enter, and despite their anguish, families began to trust the effort and respect the boundaries. A shared purpose unites people with different skills, backgrounds, and perspectives to work together.

The *network of relationships* that leaders brought to the rescue effort became the conduit for resources, information, and ideas. The effort required several teams of different specialties: drilling, ground operations, data analysis, external communications, and victim support services. There was no time to interview and build org charts. Sougarret relied on the relationships and reputations of the volunteers to assemble a leadership team for these various functions. Each of these leaders then drew on their network of professional and personal relationships. A family friend of one of the rescue operation leaders was a geologist turned entrepreneur who had improved upon existing drilling technology. Other contacts tapped the help of an Australian software company that provided the real-time data needed to correct the drilling trajectory. A phone call to a friend in Afghanistan brought expert American military drillers to the site. Outreach to rescuers for another mining disaster resulted in a collaboration between the Chilean Navy and NASA to design the rescue capsule. The relationships leaders and their teams have and develop inside and outside the organization are their greatest resource—and the more diverse those relationships, the better.

The rescue operation approached the uncertainty and volatility of the situation with *openness and curiosity*. Openness is a psychological measure of receptivity to new ideas and experiences that allows us to assess and explore the unknown. Without reliable maps of the mine, not knowing the composition of the rock, and contending with ground instability, the engineering team drilled multiple holes to develop drill profiles of the rock in the mine. Data from these test holes were analyzed by 3D mapping software to find potential trajectories to the safety refuge. Additionally, a research team was tasked to study past mining accidents. They found an event at the Quecreek Mine in Pennsylvania that shared similarities with this collapse, so they invited members of that rescue team to share their experiences and perspectives. When faced with novelty, uncertainty, or opacity of information, observation and inquiry are vital to solving a problem.

Employing *critical thinking*, rescuers challenged the assumptions of politics, the mining industry, and common knowledge to innovate a novel solution. If President Piñera had made the accepted political move and left the owners of the San José mine to run the rescue, the miners, and possibly the ill-equipped rescuers that first arrived, would have died. Sougarret could also have accepted the conclusions of the first rescue team, the Chilean Carabineros Special Operations Group, and decided that without adequate airshafts, there was no way to rescue the miners. If rescuers had accepted the assumption that safety protocols had been followed in the mine, they would have assumed the surviving miners had 30 days of supplies in the safety refuge, but in fact they only had days before they would starve to death. The chance of reaching the safety refuge using time-consuming and inaccurate drilling techniques of the mining industry was 1.25 percent. Rescuers chose to look to other industries for faster and more accurate technology informed by data analysis. In fact, the successful trajectory of the drill hole that first reached the miners was so unexpected it was initially rejected. The lead engineer had to convince the drill crew to pursue it by using a soccer analogy to explain the physics. A key component of safety capacity is possibility. Rigid and unexamined assumptions limit options for recovery from failure.

Recognizing the unknown unknowns of their mission, rescuers *experimented*, testing multiple hypotheses simultaneously. Rescuers were ridiculed in the press for all the test holes they initially drilled to gather data. Reaching the miners initially was a triumph of innovation, but creating a hole stable and large enough to get them out was a greater challenge. Because the psychological stress on the miners and their families required quick action, the rescuers chose to simultaneously test three different approaches, deemed Plan A, Plan B and Plan C. Each plan used different technologies and had different inherent risks. The rescuers calculated that the costs of testing each approach in sequence were greater than testing them simultaneously because they could stop the others once one succeeded. Plan B, the most novel method and brainchild of a 24-year-old field engineer, reached the miners first. Any new effort is an experiment. Being clear on the hypothesis and assumptions of any plan allows leaders to better understand each new uncertainty they face and improve decision-making and problem-solving.

Everything the rescuers did to create the capacity for a safe return of the miners to their families required vulnerability and *emotional resiliency*. The rescue effort at the San José Mine took a total of 69 days. An initial conventional plan, to rescue them by drilling a tunnel from a nearby accessible mine, would have taken 14 months. Innovation took great courage on the part of the rescuers. Every setback was amplified in the press as an irretrievable failure. René Aguilar, in charge of communications for the rescue, made concerted efforts to minimize the demoralizing spiral of blame. He did so by being transparent about daily progress and setbacks. All the leadership considered the emotions and psychological health of the families, the trapped miners, and the rescuers themselves in their decisions. Aguilar told an interviewer, "It was important from day one to keep reminding everyone that we are here for one purpose only—rescue trapped miners as soon as possible. We don't have time for fighting, competing, and blaming because you are risking lives by doing that." He focused on helping everyone in the operation cope with the difficult emotions of the situation simply by encouraging a compassionate environment where everyone showed care for each other. The practice of managing failure and addressing uncertainty to create the capacity to do dangerous work safely is inherently emotional and requires emotional intelligence on the part of leaders.

Safety leaders can learn from the Chilean mining rescue case what it takes to recover safety capacity, even in operations that have created unsafe conditions. Six leadership practices that build safety capacity organizationally, operationally, and psychologically are as follows:

1. Recognizing and regularly communicating the shared purpose of your team, operation, or cross-functional effort
2. Continually building and encouraging diverse and genuine relationships within and outside your organization and industry
3. Cultivating openness and curiosity to build observation and inquiry skills in yourself and your team
4. Fostering critical thinking by identifying and challenging assumptions and identifying alternatives
5. Building an experimentation practice by recognizing and formulating the hypotheses behind your decisions and actions and testing your initiatives
6. Developing emotional intelligence and practicing emotional resiliency. The following chapters will explore how leaders can bring these safety-capacity-building practices into their day-to-day leadership.

Safety Capacity Reflection Questions

What strategic pressures is your organization experiencing? Is your organization sacrificing safety capacity in its response to them, or is it building capacity? How?

1. Are there organizational weaknesses in role definition, processes and procedures, communication, and metrics that could diminish safety capacity in the operations you lead? How does your organization address these weaknesses?

2. What might be limitations to your organization's ability to identify emerging hazards and innovate effective controls and barriers? How could you address these limitations?

3. In what ways does your organizational or team culture promote or suppress openness and curiosity? To what extent are team members willing to discuss failure, speak candidly, question the status quo, express different opinions, be authentic, or ask for help?

4. Of the six leadership practices listed above, which comes most naturally to you? Which is the most challenging?

CHAPTER 2: SHAPE A SHARED PURPOSE

What's the mark of a leader? The strength to dominate others, or the willingness to be vulnerable in service of the well-being of all?

They came looking for macho men. Gender researchers from Harvard and Stanford traveled to Louisiana to study the culture of offshore oil-drilling platforms.[5] They had heard tales of men in this dangerous work environment fist-fighting each other to become the driller, the most prestigious job on the rig. They were excited to interview this pack of lions! When they arrived, they were told the stories were true, but it wasn't true anymore. Things had changed—because of a safety initiative.

The researchers interviewed workers, managers, and contractors, and they all agreed, things were different now. Their previous *macho* behaviors were no longer acceptable to them. Now they were vulnerable. One worker opened up about his daughter being shot and the others supported him and helped him stay focused when doing difficult work. Men said they appreciated being corrected because they wanted to learn and didn't fear blame or ridicule anymore. One man with many years of experience explained how he sought out the opinions of novices because they would provide a valuable and different perspective. They were focused on problem-solving rather than being the one who was right. Researchers observed workers pausing to consider different options for completing their work safely. One formally macho man told researchers, "We are a very different group now than we were when we first got together—kinder, gentler people."[6]

So how did this happen? The researchers pointed to one thing: a shared sense of purpose. The safety initiative switched these men's focus from their individual survival in a masculine hierarchy, to the shared goal of

---

[5] Robin J. Ely and Debra E. Meyerson, "Unmasking Manly Men: The Organizational Reconstruction of Men's Identity," *Academy of Management Proceedings*, vol. 2006, no. 1 (2006), https://www.hbs.edu/faculty/Pages/item.aspx?num=23730.

[6] Ely & Meyerson (2006), page 26.

ensuring everyone's well-being. They shifted from being ego driven to purpose driven. As a mechanic in the study explained: "A good day [back then] was a day that you didn't get [chewed out] for doing something wrong or being perceived as not doing enough. That was a good day. Today, a good day is when nobody gets hurt, we make our production goals—or we make as much as we can based on the limitations of safety and the operating environment—and everybody feels like they've contributed something to that."[7] The shift worked, by all measures. Recordable injuries dropped dramatically, there was a significant increase in productivity (number of barrels), efficiency (cost per barrel), and reliability (up time), and pollution levels bottomed out.

Is your organization purpose driven or ego driven?

Maybe your workers aren't trying to out-shout each other, but there are less obvious clues of ego driven behavior. Consider how they perceive their roles, approach procedures, communicate with each other, and define success. Are workers reluctant to step out of their role because it gives them power, status, and acceptance? Are they more likely to say, "That's above my paygrade," than offer a differing perspective or share a new idea? If workers encounter competing priorities or don't have the resources to complete a task, will they gut it out and struggle to meet expectations? Or will they push back, ask for help, and ask questions, even if they risk looking bad? Do leaders get unsolicited bad news? Do workers actually use the *open-door policy*, or do they struggle to figure out problems on their own so they don't get labeled a *complainer*? Will workers do anything to *hit their numbers*? Do they fear for their jobs if

---

7   Ely & Meyerson (2006), page 29.

they don't make their goals? Or do they approach these types of setbacks with curiosity and look for opportunities to improve? Fearful and defensive behavior is ego-protective. Open, vulnerable, and empathetic behavior puts purpose before self.

The good news is that humans naturally favor the well-being of the group over the protection of the ego. E. O. Wilson, the father of sociobiology, determined humans are eusocial—like termites and mole rats: they evolve to adapt to the environment by changes in their social structures, not by changes in individual organisms. This means two important things: first, we need each other to survive, and second, through cooperation, we can handle almost any adversity or take advantage of any opportunity. And the most powerful motivation for cooperation is shared purpose.

Purpose is the reason why an organization, or group of people, exists. Imagine the scene in the movie where the person at the head of the table says, "I bet you are wondering why I have called you all here." And making a lot of money isn't a compelling shared purpose. Yes, it might be what everyone in the room needs, but they need it individually, selfishly. In 2019, the Business Roundtable, a group of over 180 millionaire and billionaire CEOs, rejected the long-held notion that the purpose of business is to make money. Yes, profits matter, but profits are the outcome of a greater purpose. In their words, purpose is the *animating force* for producing profit. They went on to say that the purpose of a corporation should ultimately help various stakeholders to "lead a life of meaning and dignity."

Saying safety is a priority isn't enough either. Safety is a requisite condition for doing dangerous work. If you can do dangerous work safely, eventually you just can't do that work anymore. But why is it worth doing something that could kill you? Sure, extracting minerals out of the ground is valuable. People make a lot of money building high-rises and erecting cell towers. But how do those hazardous endeavors create meaning and dignity? There are so many ways. Lithium, oil, and copper power our modern world; we couldn't even do a Google search without them. High-rises are the pride of some of the world's most vibrant cities. And could anyone maintain relationships these days without a mobile phone? No matter what your company does, no matter how dirty the work, there is a purpose that gives the work meaning and dignity.

Purpose brings diverse roles and perspectives together and helps workers make better decisions

Consider a busy hospital. Its purpose is to help people recover from illness, infectious disease, and injury without doing further harm. To achieve this, hospitals employ workers with diverse backgrounds and training, from surgeons with decades of education and nurses with specialized training, to orderlies, aids, and janitorial staff. Doctors take an oath to do no harm and, as with nurses, are required to take continuous education that hones their skills and, in the process, re-emphasizes their purpose. In fact, hospital administrators could easily take for granted that the medical profession instills such a strong sense of purpose that there is no need to reiterate it. But consider the power hierarchy inherent in a workplace with people with such different levels of expertise. Janitors are not afforded the same deference and respect as surgeons, and their jobs are not perceived to have as much meaning and dignity. But are their jobs as important to the purpose of the hospital as the surgeons'? Yes. The hospital cannot achieve its mission under unsanitary conditions.

In this example, a busy hospital was experiencing added pressure to turn over beds quickly. There was a checklist for orderlies and janitors, which included changing out supplies, equipment, and sheets and mopping the floor. Although the checklists were completed, the incidence of infection was on the rise. As it turns out, supply chain strains meant that certain cleaning products were in short supply. As far as the janitorial staff understood, their job was to complete certain tasks as quickly as possible. Without a shared sense of purpose with the medical professionals, they didn't see certain conditions for those tasks, such as adding a sufficient amount of disinfectant to the mop water, as important as touching every corner of the room with the mop. Also, given their low status, many didn't feel their lack of adequate supplies was important, so they didn't raise the issue. If their supervisors had instilled in these workers a shared sense of purpose—helped them realize that their role was just as important to the hospital and its patients as the physicians' role—the sense of responsibility to something greater than themselves would have helped them overcome the inherent fear in speaking up.

Can you articulate your team's shared purpose?

Don't worry if you can't. I have asked this question of hundreds of leaders, and most struggle. Shared purpose is not the same as strategy, although elements of strategy can help inform it. Strategy responds to forces such as the fluctuating competitive environment, regulatory and technical shifts in your industry, evolving customer needs, and the bargaining power of suppliers, customers, and labor. Purpose is about the shared *why*. Shared purpose is not the same as individual purpose either, but they should have some connection to create meaningful work for people. Individual purpose is unique, personal, and based on one's life story. Knowing your individual purpose is important to formulating your purpose as a leader, but your leadership purpose and your team's shared purpose are not the same. You can have multiple levels of shared purpose, the big why is always important, but a particular operation has a purpose, a particular mission has a purpose. Being able to clearly articulate all these shared purposes is important to support a work environment that promotes learning and creates the capacity for safety.

To identify a shared purpose, let's start with your organization's mission and strategy. For example, Walmart's mission statement is, "We Save People Money So They Can Live Better." Their strategy for competing in their industry involves several activities, from what merchandise they choose and how they manage their supply chain to where they choose to locate stores and how they staff them. Inherent in the strategy is a value proposition, and this can be articulated as, "Everyday low prices for a broad range of goods that are always in stock in convenient geographic locations."

Now let's consider a warehouse where there are many different workers uniquely tasked to fulfill this value proposition: forklift drivers, inspectors, order pickers, clerks, etc. If you were the warehouse manager, what would you say the shared purpose of the warehouse operation is? It would be something like, "To ensure every store we serve is always stocked with what people in our community need to live better." It's important that everyone in the warehouse shares this purpose, because when they come upon competing objectives, they can more easily find agreement on what matters. For example, the forklift drivers might have an objective to maximize the use of space, but the pickers have an objective to be responsive on a daily basis to the changing stock needs of each store. How the forklift drivers organize the pallets to save space might keep the pickers from easily accessing what the stores need that day. Focusing on their shared purpose would help the forklift drivers and pickers collaborate on a pallet scheme that meets their goals and fulfills the purpose, for example, to make bottled water more accessible when hurricanes are forecasted.

How does a shared purpose build safety capacity?

Responding to strategic pressures, such as supply chain issues, or addressing operational disruptions, such as a change of operating environment, or even managing disputes between two teams, can be facilitated by uncovering and communicating a shared purpose. Take, for example, a small oil exploration company that had recently acquired a competitor and thus expanded its portfolio of oil leases into New Mexico, a state it had never worked in before. As a New Mexican, I can attest to the fact there can be a sense of culture shock going across the border into Oklahoma or Kansas, where this company had concentrated its business before, and vice versa. The leader of field operations was working with unfamiliar tribes and state and federal agencies, all of whom appeared to be hostile. Many cases illustrate how cross-organizational power struggles resulting in red tape, delays, and additional hurdles to executing work can create unsafe conditions and error-prone situations. This leader, therefore, had to build trust quickly, but couldn't rely on familiarity and shared cultural norms. Yet something had brought all these people together to stand on the same land. Despite all their disparate interests, it was this leader's job to find the purpose they shared, communicate it, and reiterate it. In this case, the shared purpose was sustainable revenue. Sustainability meant somewhat different things to different people, but it was important to everyone. Minimizing environmental impact was of varying importance to all the stakeholders, but it served everyone. Being able to continually work in the area was of greater interest to some than others. A steady stream of revenue and demand for jobs was central for others. Despite their different needs and perspectives, one purpose could unite them, and that became the foundation for trust. This trust enabled the open communication, collaboration, conflict resolution, problem-solving, and resource sharing needed to maintain safe operations and a safety culture.

Identify and communicate shared purpose as part of your regular leadership practice

So how do you, as a safety leader, build this into your work? Several of the skills I will address in future chapters will help, such as relationship building and curiosity. Nevertheless, shaping a shared purpose, like any practice, requires some consistency and discipline. Begin by listing the interactions you regularly initiate with your team members, other teams, and stakeholders. This might include communications like emails and reports, or meetings like pre-job briefs, all hands, or project updates. Now identify the audiences of these interactions. You will probably find you have more stakeholders than you previously thought. Don't forget to include yourself in this list. The next step is to capture the interests of these stakeholders (and yourself). Why are you all working together? Why is your communication or meeting of value, and what do you each want out of it?

> **Identfying Shared Purpose**
> 1. List the interactons you regularly initate with others.
> 2. Identfy the audiences of these interactons.
> 3. Capture the interests of your primary audiences.
> 4. Examine all the interests you have found and consider what higher purpose they have in common.
> 5. Get feedback.

A good place to start is to consider what they are rewarded for and what they might be punished for. You will probably have several misconceptions about their interests at first, but your initial guess will provide a basis for inquiry. Then, take the time to ask members of each stakeholder group what they care about. Finally, examine all the interests you have identified and consider what they have in common. Don't look for the lowest common denominator, but rather at the higher purpose that unites all these interests. Write it down and test it out. Compare it to the mission and vision of your organization. Does it align? If not, revise it. (Sometimes just elevating the purpose will work.) Use words that reflect the values espoused by these stakeholders. Try it out with your closest relationships in those stakeholder groups and get feedback. And when you are confident with it, use it. Start an email with it. "I'm writing to share this information because our shared purpose is *X*." Open a meeting with, "Our shared purpose in today's operation is . . ." Or just use it as an opening question: "What's our shared purpose today?" Get feedback, refine it, repeat it.

Reflecting on purpose will also improve your leadership. Your interests are the result of your specific role, your special skills, and your unique perspective arising from your life and work experiences and lessons. As a leader, you use what makes you stand out to unify groups of people and enable others to achieve their goals collectively. Finding your contribution to a shared purpose will clarify your leadership purpose, which in turn will help you guide and inspire others—and, of course, help keep them safe.

Shared Purpose Reflection Questions

1. What cultural factors in your organization drive ego-driven narratives and behaviors? What elements of your culture support a purpose-driven mindset? What can you do to influence those factors?

2. What are the specific ways you interact with your stakeholders? Is there an email you regularly send? A meeting you run daily, weekly, or monthly? Who are the audiences of the communications and interactions? List them.

3. Consider your list and reflect on their various interests. Now consider the stated mission, vision, and values of your organization. Is there a greater purpose that unites these various interests and aligns with

the mission of the organization and how it intends to achieve it? Write down a few different options.

4. What disagreements, power struggles, miscommunications, silos, and other conflicts do you encounter with and between your stakeholders? How might a shared sense of purpose help with collaboration, conflict resolution, decision making or motivation in these situations?

5. Consider your own purpose as a leader. What interests, skills, and experience make you unique? How does your uniqueness help bring others together?

CHAPTER 3: CULTIVATE NETWORKS OF RELATIONSHIPS

Is there such a thing as lone hero? Isn't there always a trusted sidekick, a network of kind strangers, and other helpers along the journey?

Sully gets all the credit. Sure, he's both humble and highly skilled in a Tom Hanks kind of way, which makes him an irresistible hero. But if you ask New York City's incident response leadership, the miracle on the Hudson was made possible by lessons learned from 9/11. For a decade since the attack, New York's Police Department and Fire Department (FDNY), port security, the US Coast Guard, the National Transportation Safety Board, and hundreds of other organizations had been engaged in a deliberate effort to build interagency relationships.[8] When captain Chesley "Sully" Sullenberger crash-landed US Airways flight 1549 in New York's Hudson River on January 15, 2009, the safety capacity to recover from the failure existed within the city's incident management system. The system wasn't directed by one organization; it was a cooperative network whose rigor was built from years of meetings, planning sessions, exercises, and field drills between federal, state, city, and private operations. This effort addressed issues that confounded earlier disasters, like first responders self-deploying without orders, integrating multiple command centers, and making decisions when key decision-makers are not on the scene. In interviews, leaders stressed that the most important factor in coordinating the efforts of so many organizations (did you notice I said *hundreds* earlier?) was the genuine relationships between counterparts. As FDNY chief of department Salvatore Cassano said in 2009, "[If] you don't talk to each other, you might as well throw the radios in the water."[9]

---

8   Jonathan Weeks, Arnold M. Howitt, and Herman B. Leonard, *Miracle on the Hudson* ©: Epilogue (Cambridge: Harvard Kennedy School, 2012), https://case.hks.harvard.edu/miracle-on-the-hudson-epilogue/.

9   Weeks, Howitt, & Leonard (2012), page 3

Organizations are systems of meaning

Organizations aren't a set of buildings, job descriptions, or org charts. They are made up of meaningful relationships. Think of the information and resources you need to do your job and lead your team. Most leaders tend to spend their time maintaining vertical relationships: those who manage them, and those they manage. But for your team to execute its work well and build the capacity to learn and recover from failure, horizontal relationships matter just as much, if not more. Dangerous work often requires specialized skills and experience. For example, the general contractor for the construction of a bridge doesn't have the skills and experience to do all the jobs and run all the equipment and machinery that each subcontractor does. The engineers, iron workers, pavers, and utility installers working on the project rely on information and resources from across the many jobs and functions involved in the project as well as information and resources from the local authorities and agencies scoping and inspecting the project. With many specialized entities coordinating their efforts, trust, communication, and collaboration are essential to problem-solving and decision-making. Merely handing off work from one subcontractor to another is a guaranteed recipe for inefficiency, delays, rework, and overruns.

It's leaders who broker the information and resources workers need to do their jobs. Leaders frame the problems workers must solve and facilitate the decisions that need to be made. Take a moment to identify your primary sources of information. Where do your resources—money, equipment, supplies, etc.—come from? Now think about the people who share that information and allocate those resources. Do you know them well? Do they care about you and your team, and are they invested in your success? When facing a failure, would you turn to them for help? Do you trust them enough to be vulnerable and admit you are concerned about the safety of the operation? If any of these questions make you uncomfortable, you might consider how to improve the quality of these relationships.

Now consider a thorny problem your team might encounter, one that would require novel information, additional resources, or innovative ideas to solve well. Who would you or your team reach out to for help? Would they have broad experience and therefore a strategic view of the issue? Would they be able to provide a unique or outside perspective? Would they be willing to invest in finding the best solution even though they are not closely tied to your team? If not, you might want to broaden and diversify your network of support and find ways to build understanding and connection with people who are not like you.

What barriers does your team run up against when making and executing decisions? Does it need to build consensus with other people who share a stake in those decisions? Do team members need to better understand the consequences of their decisions, either across stakeholders or in the future? Could your team's decisions make or break a strategy your organization is relying upon to succeed? If the answer to any of these questions is yes, you may want to start thinking about developing sponsorship and mentorship relationships for your team. Sponsors champion your team's decisions and initiatives and provide opportunities, while mentors help improve decision-making by facilitating learning. How do you find sponsors and mentors? Let's start by specifically addressing how to establish, improve, diversify, and develop relationships that are advantageous to safety.

Improve the quality of your relationships

Good relationships are built on trust, not persuasion or likeability. Interdependency can breed contempt if genuine trust isn't built. Consider the relationship Boeing employees had with the Federal Aviation Administration (FAA) when certifying the highly problematic 737 Max aircraft.[10] Five years before the newly launched 737 Max 8 crashed twice, killing 346 people, and ten years before serious production issues were discovered after a door plug detached mid-flight on a 737 Max 9, electronic communications revealed deep veins of mistrust and deceit. A Boeing employee referred to FAA regulators as "dogs watching TV" when describing a presentation to convince said regulators to certify the aircraft. Another Boeing employee said they had to use "Jedi mind tricks" to persuade regulators. But investigations later showed that the FAA was inclined to be beyond lenient with Boeing. Afterall, Boeing's success had a huge impact on the American aviation industry. Similarly, communications from Boeing provided examples of contempt for the airlines who purchased the planes, calling pilots that would need simulator training on the 737 Max "idiots," even though when asked, they admitted they would not let a family member fly on a plane whose pilot had not received simulator training.

The Boeing employees had a shared purpose with their regulators and customers but viewed these stakeholders as adversaries. Persuasion is a tool of conquest. Although it doesn't necessarily require deception, it drives an agenda. Consider common persuasion techniques: scarcity ("Act now before it's too late!"); making a favorable contrast ("Yes, this

---

10 David Gelles, "'I Honestly Don't Trust Many People at Boeing': A Broken Culture Exposed," *The New York Times*, 2020, https://www.nytimes.com/2020/01/10/business/boeing-737-employees-messages.html.

technology is safer, but look how expensive it is. Is it worth it?"); or social pressure ("None of our other customers need this training."). Driving an agenda fosters mistrust. There are many trust models produced by consultants and scholars, but one thing they all have in common is this: *if someone believes you have their best interest at heart, they will trust you*. If they consider you to be self-interested, even if you are offering something valuable, they will not trust you. How do you indicate that you have their interests at heart? Ask questions and listen. Find out what they care about. Share what you care about even if it is a competing interest, and negotiate in transparency.

Honesty trumps liking. It's an established psychological bias that people are more generous to people they like. You may have been told to find common interests like kids, cars, or sports to build relationships with people. Absolutely, that is a great way to find someone to hang out with, but friends are not necessarily going to help you build safety capacity. In fact, they might serve to reduce it. Relying on a network of friends for information, resources, and learning will ultimately narrow your perspective because *like likes like*. In other words, you are unlikely to access broad possibilities from relationships with people just like yourself. What matters is trust. Do you trust everyone you like? I'm sure you can think of a close friend you would never loan your truck to or never rely on to pick up your kid or pet from daycare on time. Trust is based on different assessments than liking. Do you think this person is capable and skilled to do what they say they are going to do and meet their commitments? Do you think they have the integrity to do the right thing even if it means putting themselves at risk? And this needn't be a running into a burning building level of risk. It can be as simple as risking the embarrassment of saying, "I was wrong." Finally, when you disagree with them, do you believe they are arguing from their genuine opinion, or just trying to win?

Wouldn't you rather build the relationships you rely on to keep workers safe on commitment, consistency, and compassion than steak dinners and hockey games?

Broaden and diversify your relationships

Enlisting and developing ambassadors increases the scope of your network. At this point you may be anxious about the prospect of having to maintain an unmanageable number of relationships with people you respect but don't enjoy spending time with. Thankfully, building safety capacity with a network of relationships is not all on you as the leader. You can borrow the trust built by people on your team and in your network to expand the influence of your team or function. One of the benefits of recruiting a diverse team and concentrating on building a few genuine relationships with people different from you is that it multiplies your ability to get the information, resources, and help your team or function needs to learn and improve.

Many studies have underscored the importance of escaping the silos that form in organizations. A study of senior-level professionals at a global professional services firm compared men with similar credentials: same amount of time with the firm, same department, same graduation year, same number of annual hours billed.[11] Professionals who communicated mainly along their chain of command and within their department produced *one-quarter of the profitability and growth* than professionals who actively reached outside their silos and developed relationships with

---

11   Heidi K. Gardner, Smart Collaboration: *How Professionals and Their Firms Succeed by Breaking Down Silos* (Boston: Harvard Business Review Press, 2016), https://hbsp.harvard.edu/product/10001-PDF-ENG.

colleagues who also had broad networks. Let me say this again: those who kept their professional relationships close worked just as much as those who broadened the scope of their relationships, but they got one-fourth of the reward for their efforts. Comparing the siloed network maps against the broad ones, it's striking that, although the more successful professionals did communicate with more people, it's not significantly more. The most noticeable difference was that the people they chose to communicate with had a great deal of connections themselves. Those well-connected people are ambassadors for you, your team, and your function. By well-connected, I do not mean high-status social butterflies. I mean people who, maybe by function of their role, interact with people across functions or stakeholder groups. They might also be well-connected by virtue of the trust and knowledge they have built within a certain function or among certain stakeholders. So maybe their relationships aren't that broad, but they are meaningful, and they can be your *insider* to a group you wouldn't get to know on your own.

You can either find or create ambassadors. Look to the people you lead and influence. How might you help them build the relationships they need to learn and improve? Is there someone on your team who has a skill another group could use? Is there an operation that feeds into yours that could create problems if they don't produce what you expect? Why not send someone to learn their process and get to know that team? How about creating visibility for team members with important stakeholders such as regulators, suppliers, union representatives, or higher-ups? You don't always have to be the point of contact. Encouraging individual team members to develop horizontal and vertical relationships strengthens the whole team.

Even if you do not formally manage a team, you can turn your boss and colleagues into ambassadors for you and the safety function. Consider how they might help build a bridge between you and a group you have little influence over. Or maybe they can help translate their needs and interests for you so that you can better build trust with a group or function you have been at odds with. What's important is to develop a network of relationships where you are no more than a degree or two away from those who have vital information or resources or make decisions that impact safety.

Secure sponsorship and mentorship for you and your team

Sponsors give you opportunities, and mentors help you prepare for those opportunities. Sponsorship and mentorship are terms usually raised in career-development discussions, so let me explain why this is important to safety. At the turn of the 21st century (that sounds weird!), when I started working in the nuclear field, I had the opportunity to benchmark nuclear power plants with the Department of Energy, and I first became exposed to Human Performance. The revelation that changed how the nuclear industry viewed safety arose from the observation that nearly every incident investigation found the root cause to be human error. Once they recognized that humans make decisions in a context of meaning created by social and organizational systems, then investigators started to uncover the organizational weaknesses, hazardous conditions, and error-prone situations that the humans making the errors had to navigate. They realized, in most cases, that the decisions previously labeled erroneous made perfect sense within this context. To shape the context in which workers are making decisions, you need sponsors. To help workers navigate and interpret the organizational systems that shape their work, they need mentors.

With respect to safety, sponsors are generally senior-level decision-makers who can include you or members of your team or function in organizational decisions. Is your organization thinking about implementing a gross-margin management program? You want someone who understands how this will affect workers to inform the decisions around the structure and implementation of that program. Is your organization procuring electric vehicles or other new equipment? Workers who will drive those vehicles and use that equipment have valuable information that may be the difference between that change creating an error-prone situation or not. You will need a sponsor to bring the workers' concerns and considerations to the table. Procurement, human resources, senior management—they don't want to make decisions in a silo, but it's just easier sometimes. To elevate safety considerations to these levels, you need to create channels of communication between the field, the floor, or the lab and the offices. So you need to find sponsors who will say, "Let's bring a machinist onto the investigation," or, "Let's pilot the new program in the Springfield plant," or, "Before we purchase, let's invite a few drivers to test it out."

Mentors have an ongoing relationship with you and members of your team. Mentors can become sponsors when an important initiative is proposed or a decision is being made. But to be prepared when these situations arise, you must cultivate mentor relationships that facilitate continuous learning. Asking a manager to mentor a frontline worker helps the manager understand how their decisions influence the work and helps the worker understand how their everyday choices make or break the strategy of the organization. It's a reciprocal relationship, so mentors needn't be senior-level people. Let's say one of your industrial safety engineers doesn't have much familiarity with a particular process or operation. You might ask a worker who has done that operation frequently or in different contexts to mentor the engineer. A success factor for mentorship is start with a clear objective at first: "Could Becky shadow you this week so she can learn about the steps you take and why?" Also encourage casual interactions: "Becky should get to know the team. Can she join you all for lunch?" Remember, one genuine relationship can foster trust across organizational boundaries, so think about how to make mentor relationships meaningful.

How do relationships build safety capacity?

Building a strong and diverse network of relationships is essential to maintaining and improving safety capacity at the psychological, operational, and organizational levels. All three levels are interconnected by information, resources, perceptions, and decisions that are communicated (or not) across a network of human relationships. Transparency across these networks of relationships between workers, leaders, functions, departments, and external stakeholders, like regulators, ensures that good decisions are made, unintended consequences are minimized, and the organization can recover from failure. Such transparency depends on trust. All organizations have internal competition for resources, information, and visibility, and this creates power dynamics, which (like all politics) are best navigated through relationships. Who you know determines what you get to do. Organizations that do hazardous work are increasingly complex because they need workers with specific expertise and experience, must operate under various types of regulation, and increasingly utilize technology (either to better control the materials or other hazards they work with, or because the work is expensive or exacting to execute). We can't simplify complexity, but we can make it more manageable by focusing on the interdependencies between different teams, functions, and types of expertise (*tight couplings*, if you want to get nerdy). In human systems, all those interdependencies are facilitated by relationships between people. Manage the relationships to manage the complexity.

Cultivate networks of relationships as part of your regular leadership practice

Extraverts think they are great at networking, but the social butterfly approach tends to result in a lot of superficial acquaintanceships and will likely miss some important strategic relationships. Introverts hate networking, but you don't have to gladhand at conferences or make small talk in the cafeteria line to build the relationships you and your team need. In fact, I have noticed that being an introvert has its advantages when networking. It's not necessary for me to like someone to engage with them on a topic or project that matters to me. Similarly, I have found that I don't need someone to like me for me to be motivated to do a good job and help them the best I can. Because I'm uncomfortable talking about myself to strangers, I ask a lot of questions, and people respond well to that. Nevertheless, whether you are introverted or extroverted, it's best to have a plan.

<u>Begin by assessing your existing network of relationships</u>. You may want to pull your team together to do this. Start with the most important operation your team executes, and think about the most difficult or dangerous activities in that operation. If the team lacks information or encounters ambiguous information with respect to these activities, who do they go to for clarity? What about the resources needed for this operation—who makes the resource allocation decisions? Who else has input into decisions upstream that could have an impact on the operation? List the people your team most relies on in these areas. Try to list at least half a dozen if you can.

Look at the list and rate the quality of the relationship with each person on a scale of 1-10, with 10 being "best working relationship ever" and 1 being "why are they ghosting us?" Consider things such as: is there give and take in the relationship? Do you trust them enough to admit a mistake? Do they trust you enough to give you bad news? Once you have rated the quality, determine what value each person adds to your team. Categorize the value they bring in one of the following four categories: information availability, resource availability, subject matter expertise, or decision-making authority. Someone in the first category provides you with the information you need for the operation, information about other groups and the larger organization, or even intelligence on resource availability, subject matter experts, or decision-makers. Someone with resource availability can give you money, equipment, people, or access to a shared resource like a particular lab or building. A person with subject matter expertise might know a lot about your operation or some aspect of it, like a specific technology. They might also be particularly good at solving problems. Finally, decision-making authorities are people who can allow or disallow something that is critical to your operation. After you have determined what value these relationships offer, you will plot their proximity to you. Create four concentric circles, with *Same Team* in the center, *Different Team* in the next ring outside that, *Different Department* as the next outer ring, and *Different Organization* as the furthest outer ring. Divide the concentric circles into quadrants, and label the four sections *Information Availability*, *Resource Availability*, *Subject Matter Expertise*, and *Decision-Making Authority*. Plot the names (you may want to use initials) with their quality ratings in their appropriate quadrant and at the distance they are from your team. You can put someone in different quadrants if they provide more than one type of value to your team.

CULTIVATE NETWORKS OF RELATIONSHIPS

Now reflect on your network map. Is everyone clustered near your team, so that you are working in an echo chamber? If so, you'll need to develop relationships outside of your silo. Are all four quadrants populated? If not, you will need to identify people who can help you in the areas where you are lacking. Are some or many of your relationships rated below 5? Is there a particular quadrant with low-quality relationships? It's time to start working on building trust. Discuss the map with your team and make an action plan. Find sponsors with decision-making authority and mentors with subject matter expertise. Ask contacts with information availability to introduce you to their sources. Provide opportunities for members of your team to mentor those with resources about the importance of your operations and its critical needs. Developing a healthy network of relationships will take time, but it's a worthwhile investment.

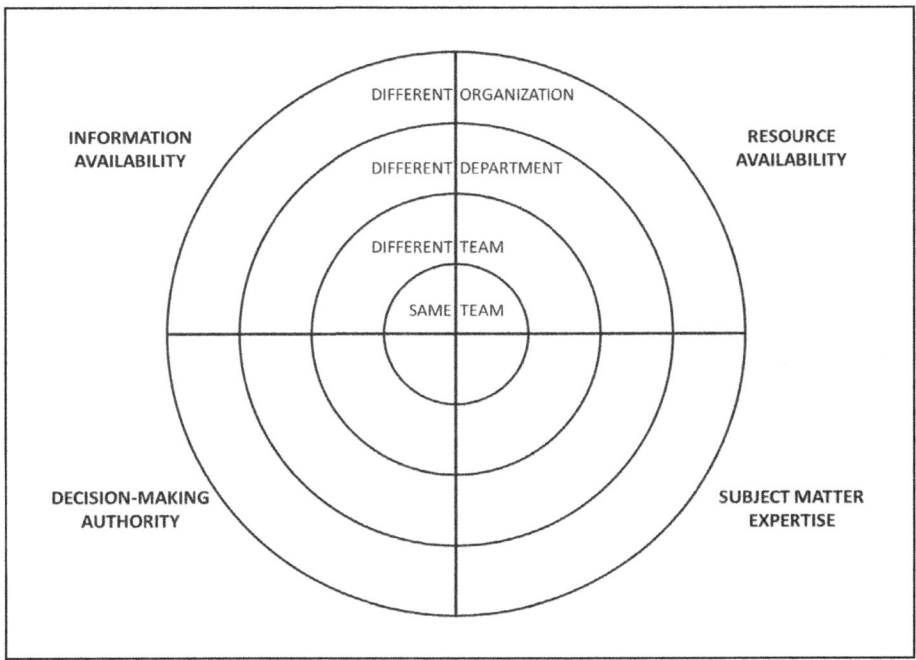

Figure 2: Relationship Network Map

Relationship Networks Reflection Questions

1. Who do you rely on for the information, resources, and decisions you and your team need to do work safely and meet your goals? Do you know them well? Are they invested in your success? When facing a failure, would you turn to them for help? If you have any doubts, what can you do to improve the quality of the relationship by building trust?

2. Think about the most challenging problems you and your team face. Do you know people who can offer a different perspective, share broad experiences, and communicate strategic considerations? If not, how can you find them? If so, how do you strengthen and maintain those relationships?

3. Consider the barriers your team runs up against when either making and executing decisions or needing a key stakeholder to make a decision. In what way could a sponsor help? What decision-makers and decision-making processes would you most want your team to have access to?

4. What would you like your stakeholders to understand about your team and their work? How could you create opportunities for team members to mentor others outside the team?

5. Consider the process outlined in this chapter for mapping your network of relationships. Who do you need to include in the process? How will you roll out the improvements to your identified network?

CHAPTER 4: FOSTER OPENNESS AND CURIOSITY

A study shows that openness to new ideas and experiences is more important to patient safety than disclosing and reducing medical errors. Could it be that learning is more important than getting everything right?

CHAPTER 4: FOSTER OPENNESS AND CURIOSITY

Sir Robert Francis was concerned that hundreds, perhaps thousands, of patients were dying in the English National Health Service (NHS) each year as a result of poor standards of care.[12] He chaired a study in 2013 that hypothesized that medical errors, hospital safety standards, and low morale among staff were likely culprits. The Francis Inquiry, as it was called, observed among doctors and other medical staff a sense of helplessness and lack of transparency that resulted from fear of blame and repercussions. In 2016, the NHS launched the independent Healthcare Safety Investigation Branch in response to the Francis Inquiry. One of its initiatives measured the level of openness among hospital staff. *Openness* is a standardized psychological measure of receptivity to new ideas and experiences. Researchers, seeking to substantiate the finding of the Francis Inquiry, analyzed data from 137 hospitals. The results surprised them. A mere one-point increase in the standardized openness score among staff was associated with a *6.48 percent reduction in hospital mortality rates.* Openness also had a much stronger effect on mortality reduction than reducing error (a 1.69 percent decrease in mortality) or disclosing error (a 1.25 percent decrease).

Errors are normal

This is one of the five principles of Human and Organizational Performance (HOP).[13] Although medical errors can certainly lead to bad outcomes, focusing on the elimination of errors, as the study above suggests, isn't

---

12 Veronica Toffolutti and David Stuckler, "A Culture of Openness Is Associated with Lower Mortality Rates Among 137 English National Health Service Acute Trusts," *Health Affairs* 38, no. 5 (2019): 844-850, https://www.healthaffairs.org/doi/10.1377/hlthaff.2018.05303.

13 Todd E. Conklin, *The 5 Principles of Human Performance: A Contemporary Update of the Building Blocks of Human Performance for the New View of Safety* (2019), https://www.amazon.com/Principles-Human-Performance-contemporary-updateof/dp/1794639144.

necessarily going to eliminate said bad outcomes. What matters is how we recover from errors, and that's safety capacity. Openness creates the capacity to recover from failure by raising awareness of opportunities to improvise. Openness can be described as a "yes, and" mindset, like that of improv theater. Beginning with "yes" allows the mind to accept and appreciate the situation we are presented with. "And" implores us to be curious and consider what *might be*. In other words, "and" considers how we might add value to the situation and make it better.

A simultaneously triumphant and tragic example of improvisation to recover from failure is the Mann Gulch fire of 1949. Science journalist Malcolm Gladwell describes it as an example of intuitive innovation, while psychologist Karl Weick considers it a failure of group sensemaking. On August 5, 1949, in Montana, twelve US Forest Service (USFS) firefighters died, and a critical lifesaving technique was developed, which firefighters still use today.[14] Wag Dodge was the highly experienced and respected foreman of a crew of young smokejumpers, some of whom were rookies, most of whom had never worked with him before. He and his crew descended into Mann Gulch laden with tools to dig trenches to control a forest fire. But with wind gusts up to 40 miles an hour, the fire quickly blew up and raced toward the men, blocking their planned escape route to the river. Upon seeing the situation, Dodge ordered his men to drop their tools and retreat from the fire. Many of the men did not. Then Dodge realized they could not outrun the fire, so he lit a fire in a small area near them to clear a space free of fuel to shelter until the fire passed. No one in the USFS had ever lit what is now known as an *escape fire* before. When Dodge beckoned crew members to join him in the scorched terrain he

---

14   Michael A. Roberto and Elena M. Ferlins, *Fire at Mann Gulch* (Boston: Harvard Business School, 2003).https://hbsp.harvard.edu/product/304089-PDF-ENG.

had created, no one followed his lead. One survivor said it seemed like a good idea, but for what, he didn't know. So Dodge lay down alone in his scorched refuge, breathing into a handkerchief, and survived. Others ran past him and died.

Certainty is the enemy of learning

Wag Dodge realized the conditions he and his crew encountered were untenable. Without deliberation, he accepted the situation and applied his experience in a novel way. He knew how fire worked, and even though he had never been in a predicament like that before, he figured out a solution. He learned. He took one model of understanding and applied it to a different context and produced something different and enhanced. Yet, he couldn't quickly teach his crew this new technique in a way they could get it and follow his lead. Why? Robert Sallee, a surviving crew member who was only 17 when he jumped into Mann Gulch, gave an interview to *Outside* magazine in 1995, saying: "The problem today is that when you teach people to fight fire, they go into it expecting to win."[15] Smokejumpers in the 1940s and today are considered an elite group. Norman Maclean wrote in his book *Young Men and Fire*: "In 1949 the Smokejumpers were still so young that they referred affectionately to all fires as *ten o'clock fires*, as if they already had them under control before they jumped."[16] Apparently, a common boast among this group was that they could dig a trench around any fire by ten in the morning. This mindset is not open to the possibility of failure. It doesn't allow for acceptance of an unexpected

---

15 Roberto & Ferlins (2003), page 9

16 Roberto & Ferlins (2003), page 2

situation, nor does it consider the possibility of doing things differently when faced with change.

Safety has been relying on "no, don't" instead of "yes, and" for too long

Unfortunately, organizations are reluctant to encourage a mindset of "yes, and"—especially with respect to safety. There's a fear of inefficiency, mistakes, and poor performance. But improvisation doesn't mean being unprepared. In fact, it means being prepared for many eventualities. Trying to create safety by proceduralizing complex work only reduces a worker's capacity to respond to emerging hazards. Procedures create the illusion of consistency and drive confirmation bias. Attempting to write a procedure that covers all eventualities won't protect workers any better. Despite many efforts, no one can predict the future. Not that you shouldn't consider many eventualities and identify controls and barriers for potential hazards. To help workers become curious about what might happen, a collaborative discussion of the unexpected is much more effective than a static document. Kevin Dunbar at the University of Maryland studied lab researchers conducting experiments. Although scientists are supposed to be curious, human nature is driven by expectation—we tend to see what we want to see—and these researchers were not immune to confirmation bias. But what startled Dunbar was that these scientists didn't just ignore unexpected results.[17] Finding what they didn't expect resulted in activity in the dorsolateral prefrontal cortex, the brain's Delete button. The key to recognizing an emergent situation is to encourage workers' curiosity and create an expectation for the unexpected.

---

17 Fugelsang, Jonathan A., and Kevin N. Dunbar. "Brain-based mechanisms underlying complex causal thinking." Neuropsychologia 43, no. 8 (2005): 1204-1213, https://www.sciencedirect.com/science/article/abs/pii/S002839320400274X

Researchers at Harvard Business School measured the curiosity of 250 people who had just started new jobs.[18] There was variation among the scores based on their personalities, as expected. But when the researchers retested the group after six months of doing the same job, they found that, controlling for the variability due to personality, curiosity dropped by nearly 20 percent. They attributed the drop to valuing productivity over learning. Although these workers needed to learn about their new jobs, once they performed adequately, they felt pressure not to ask questions or explore opportunities for improvement. A common sentiment was that there "just isn't time for that." Dangerous work requires more curiosity about the unexpected, unintended, and uncertain, yet it experiences the same performance pressures as any other mission-critical work. To counter natural and unconscious human tendencies to normalize hazards, change, and drift in practices, leaders must create more opportunities for operational learning.

Encourage inquiry over advocacy

Plan-of-the-day briefs and pre-job and post-job huddles are excellent safety practices . . . if they are forums for inquiry (or questioning) instead of advocacy (or telling). If you approach these meetings with an advocacy mindset, that is, with the idea that you are telling workers what they need to do to be safe, then you tend to defend your position, dismiss alternative perspectives, and seek to persuade others to do things in your preconceived "right way." An advocacy mindset discounts the experience of the worker and narrows the perception of the context they are working in that day. Saying something like, "Just stick to the procedure and

---

18   Peter Cappelli et al., *The New Rules of Talent Management*, Harvard Business Publication English, 2018, https://hbsp.harvard.edu/product/R1805B-PDF-ENG.

you'll be okay," won't help workers problem solve with safety as a top consideration. It tells them, "Don't problem solve, don't think; we've done the thinking for you."

An inquiry approach sets workers up to be critical thinkers and scan for the unexpected. In plan-of-the-day or pre-job meetings, instead of asking workers to confirm the plan, challenge the team to explain why certain precautions are being taken: "We are using fall protection for this job today, and it usually isn't required. Why do you think we've chosen to do that?" In post-jobs, encourage and reward workers for identifying new conditions, drifts in practices, and other changes. You might ask: "Have you noticed that the equipment is handling differently at this temperature?"

Developing an inquiry mindset in your teams will motivate creating more learning opportunities. Periodically pull together developmental learning teams rather than just post-event learning teams. Ask them to identify trends that might impact operations and consider how to adapt safely in different scenarios. For example, they may identify that a key supply item is more difficult to get or has become more expensive. They might imagine three different scenarios: (1) We must try to make do with less; (2) We get a new supplier, but the item is slightly different; and (3) We must substitute the item with something entirely different, effectively making do without it. Ask them: "How might these changes affect the safety of operations, and how can we adapt without compromising safety?" You will notice that these recommendations infuse proactive and broad inquiry into existing safety practices. You might fear that you are wasting time or driving tangential conversations, but the additional minutes in a meeting or the added meeting in a quarter could save the costs and time of attempting to recuperate from an incident.

Set learning goals aligned with performance goals

Learning isn't just about acquiring knowledge. After all, have you really learned something if you haven't changed your behavior, your attitude, or your thinking? At work, we generally engage in learning activities with the aim of realizing an opportunity or addressing a challenge. Our performance goals implicitly assume an improvement, but rarely do we explicitly identify what we need to learn to achieve this improvement. This is the origin of the classic tension between performance pressure and safety, but that tension falls away when we recognize that safety involves integrating conscious learning into our operations. Instead, we often leave workers to figure out on their own how to adapt to variable environments under the pressure of meeting performance targets, driving drift in work practices and ad hoc workarounds.

Whether you supervise workers or not, safety leadership includes discussing performance and how it will be achieved. Workers are set up to fail if they are given performance goals without the resources needed to achieve them. One important resource for change is the opportunity to learn. If you ask someone to do something differently, first recognize what they are doing now and determine the gap between the current activity and the desired performance. Considering the gap, ask whether the individual needs different knowledge, skills, and attitude (including motivation) to make the change. Maybe the organization needs to learn instead of, or in addition to, the person. Think about how the people who create the context for the work might shift their behaviors to support this new way of working. Inquire as to what knowledge, skills, and attitudes are required to do it. I'm not saying you need to create a training program, not at all. I'm saying you just need to have a coaching conversation and establish learning goals that support performance goals.

Just as you measure performance goals, you must establish how you will know that learning is happening. Performance is the lagging indicator of learning, but leading indicators serve as motivators of improvement. Nothing is more motivational to human beings than progress. Unfortunately, learning is not linear. The mistakes and confusion inherent in the learning process are essential, but they can be demotivating. So, check in on the learning. Was the document you sent opened? Did they complete the on-the-job training (OJT)? Or just ask, "How's it going? What makes sense and what doesn't?" The social aspect of learning is important. The best way to learn something is to teach it. So, make your learning goals collective, where the goal relies on interacting with someone else. It could be interacting with new people at a conference or an industry webinar. If your learning goals can bring out outside perspectives, all the better.

Disrupt the learning curve

I mentioned that learning is not linear. Indeed, it follows an S-curve. The S describes your level of performance over time. Imagine drawing an S with your finger starting from the bottom. At first the curve travels down. If that fall is drastic, we call that a *steep learning curve*. This is what people experience when there is a lot of change required for them to meet the performance requirements. This drop is necessary. There is no way to learn something new without being confused, making a mistake, or suffering some discomfort. Studies have shown that those dreaded pop quizzes you likely hated in school are a great way to learn.[19] If you loved them, you probably weren't learning; here's why. When you miss a question, your limbic brain (or your instinctual brain) reacts in pain and stimulates your

---

19   Henry L. Roediger III, Brigid Finn, "The Pluses of Getting It Wrong," Scientific American, 2010, https://www.scientificamerican.com/article/the-pluses-of-getting-it-wrong/.

hippocampus (part of your limbic brain), which is the seat of long-term memory. When the teacher gives you the right answer, your limbic brain feels rewarded, and your hippocampus holds tight to that knowledge in memory. So, if you were someone who aced pop quizzes, you were just recalling what you already knew or making a good, educated guess. Not that I would discount the self-esteem benefits of being the seventh-grade quiz master, but learning something new involves at least a little pain to get the benefit. You likely did your suffering and got your reward while diligently completing your homework.

After the learning curve dips down, it enjoys the ride up in performance. But that improvement doesn't last forever. Eventually the performance plateaus and soon declines. Recovering from the decline is tough. People are demotivated by the lack of progress and improvement, frustrated with the circumstances that hindered them (basically the changes in the work or the environment that rendered their expertise less useful), or both. When workers are in performance decline, it is the worst time to ask them to take the performance hit of learning something new. Learning is rewarding on many levels, but in many organizations, it is seen as punishment. The reason for this is that we wait too long to learn.

So don't wait. Drive learning when performance is still improving. Do this in a motivational way by cultivating curiosity about the unexpected, future threats and opportunities, adjacent technologies, etc. The practice of scanning for changes, as described above, is a great way to identify opportunities to learn. Job rotation, ad hoc projects, stretch assignments, mentoring, teach-backs—all these activities encourage workers to learn something when they are peaking in performance. In high-hazard environments, we tend to hesitate to use these development activities that are commonly used elsewhere because we are afraid to push the safety envelope. But if your safety envelope relies on people always knowing exactly the right thing to do, your envelope is dangerously thin. This sort of work disruption, like having somebody do a different job than they usually do, can significantly build your safety capacity in many ways. Not only are you creating redundancy and abundance in your workforce, but you are also exposing an activity to a new set of critical eyes and developing works with broader and more flexible skill sets.

How do openness and curiosity create safety capacity?

Have you heard about Todd Conklin's blue line and black line? The black line is work as planned: work as it is idealized in a procedure. It's flat and straight and doesn't deviate over time. I would argue that most business leaders would expect this line to slope upward, that is, for the work productivity or quality to improve over time. Regardless, the black line isn't reality. Real work is the blue line, and it's all over the place. It dips and rises as workers adapt or fail to adapt to new performance expectations, changing conditions, and surprise hazards. The blue line is actually a bunch of little learning curves: the line goes up when workers have

Before startng work:
1. What has changed since we last did this work?
2. How might this upcoming work be different?
3. What aren't we ready for?

Afer completng work:
1. Did you encounter anything surprising and unexpected?
2. Did anything make this job more difficult than expected?
3. Could a new worker do the job right following the existng procedure?

innovated something useful and drops down when they encounter something their knowledge and skills have not prepared them for. The line people don't mention as often is Todd's red line. The red line is what safety leaders are most concerned about. The red line is the hazards that are present in the work. Sure, controls for hazards are written into procedures, but like the black line, the red line in procedures is imagined—it's flat and straight. The real red line is just as bumpy as the blue line—not because the hazards are learning (unless the hazard is an evil AI), but because dangerous work happens in complex environments and complexity produces uncertainty. For example: the work area is usually dry, but the building flooded, and now workers are doing electrical in a wet environment. Or work slowed down last week due to a supply chain issue, but now we are up and running—and the production deadlines haven't changed. Or there's a new supplier for a specialized pressure gasket, and now it looks just like all the other ordinary gaskets. You get the picture. In Todd's model, the space between the blue line and the red line is safety capacity. When they meet—BOOM—there's an incident. Keeping the two lines apart requires workers and their leaders to be open to new ideas, curious about what might happen, and able to learn and change. In other words, they need a "yes, and" mindset. The "yes" has them scanning for changes that might move the red line or drive the blue line in the wrong direction. The "and" prepares them to learn ahead of challenges and move the blue line proactively rather than reactively, maintaining healthy space between work and hazard.

Foster openness and curiosity as part of a regular leadership practice

To instill openness and curiosity as a persistent mindset, I suggest a few regular practices. First, <u>turn your meetings (one-on-ones, pre-jobs, post-jobs, lessons learned, project updates, etc.) into opportunities to</u>

ask questions instead of just a way to reinforce procedures and provide solutions. Three important questions to ask workers before starting work are: (1) What has changed since we last did this work? (2) How might this upcoming work be different? (3) What aren't we ready for? These questions prompt workers and supervisors to scan for changes. After completing work, ask workers to reflect on normal operations with questions like: (1) Did you encounter anything surprising and unexpected? (2) Did anything make this job more difficult than it should have been? (3) If someone new had to do this job tomorrow, what would a veteran of the job need to show them (that's not written in the procedure) so they could do the job right?

The second practice is to never give a performance objective without identifying the gap between the current performance and the desired performance and determining what learning or other deliberate change is required to close that gap. I'm not talking just about job performance objectives—like a worker moving from being an apprentice to a journeyman—where you identify gaps by a change in task type and complexity. The new performance objective could be the expectation that because temps are rising, there will be more electrical service calls. We tend to assume that workers will just magically adapt to the increased pressure to perform, but successful and safe adaptation arises from thinking critically and consciously changing with the consideration of safety. So, for example, anticipating a surge in electrical service calls, take time to identify what worked and didn't work last summer. What might be different about this summer? What do workers need to learn to implement best practices, address potential problems, or even innovate new methods?

It's also important to <u>create learning opportunities even if performance objectives aren't changing</u>. Much of the safety capacity in operations resides in your workers' own skills, abilities, motivation, and emotional resilience. Studies consistently show that people are motivated by progress—not easy progress, but hard-won progress where they see the fruits of their efforts. Learning opportunities like cross-training and teach-backs encourage an inquiry mindset and openness and disrupt the declining end of the learning curve. So, make it a development practice to let workers pursue interests. Perhaps a computer-savvy lab technician could spend some time looking "under the hood" of your management systems with the IT department. Or your most respected engineer could learn how to coach others. It could start with a question as simple as, "What do you enjoy most about your job?"

Finally, if it's more important to be right than it is to learn in your organization, you need to change that. Most leaders (and I have asked hundreds about this) consider themselves problem-solvers, so they enter into conversations with workers with a mindset of making everything right for them, fixing the issues they are encountering, and providing the answers. Stop that! *The psychological desire to be right is the enemy of an open and curious mindset.* It can be difficult to ask questions, patiently wait for people to consider the question, and accept an answer you didn't expect and wouldn't have given. Just remember, you can't do their work for them, so you shouldn't think for them either.

Openness and Curiosity Reflection Questions

1. Think of a time when you had a chance to achieve something you wanted, but the outcome was uncertain and not fully in your control. How did you feel about the uncertainty? Was it exciting or terrifying?

Did the level of uncertainty keep you from taking that chance? If not, what did you do to manage the discomfort of the uncertainty (for example: plan for different scenarios)? If you didn't take the chance, what would have helped you decide to do it?

2. List the different interactions you have with your team and individual team members. For each of those interactions, think of a question you can open with that will drive curiosity about changes, possibilities, and uncertainties.

3. Write down the three most important performance goals for you and your team. What do you need to learn to meet or exceed those goals? How might you create opportunities to learn those things?

4. Reflect on the work your team does routinely. Who would you consider masters of certain operations or tasks? In other words, if you had to demonstrate that work to a group of VIPs, who would you want to do it? Now consider how you might challenge those workers. For example, is there a problem you might enlist them to help solve? Could they teach others? Is there a new skill, operation, or equipment you could help them learn?

CHAPTER 5: DRIVE CRITICAL THINKING

John F. Kennedy regretted his decision to invade the Bay of Pigs, but was it a poor executive decision, or a poor execution of decision-making?

CHAPTER 5: DRIVE CRITICAL THINKING

The Bay of Pigs Invasion is considered a Cold War fiasco and a breakdown of critical thinking.[20] After the American-supported invasion of Cuba failed in April of 1961, President Kennedy reportedly said, "How could I have been so stupid to let them go ahead?"[21] In a conversation with the president about the operation, General MacArthur reassured him that he had learned an important lesson: to be skeptical of expert advice with relatively small-scale (but not insignificant) consequences—death of 114 American-trained Cuban exiles, $53 million paid to Castro in ransom, the millions of dollars expended in the operation, and the real threat of war with the Soviet Union. What can we learn about critical thinking from the fiasco? First, recognize that emerging changes in the situation require a reassessment of assumptions and presumed outcomes. Second, understand that power dynamics and a lack of psychological safety keep people from speaking up about concerns and limit the way they express their true thoughts. Finally, avoid structuring decision-making as a competition between set solutions. Instead of either/or thinking, develop both/and solutions from multiple alternatives and perspectives. Resist the pressure to "solution find" by creating structured opportunities to truly problem solve.

Continually reassess assumptions and presumed outcomes in the face of change

New Mexico is often considered the last bastion of the Wild West in the United States. Even in my gentrified neighborhood in downtown Santa Fe, we still talk about a gunfight in the late 1970s between outlaws and the sheriff, in which the outlaws won the right to rule everything west of

---

20   Stephen Bates and Jack L. Rosenbloom, "Kennedy and the Bay of Pigs," (Cambridge: Kennedy School of Government, 1998), https://hbsp.harvard.edu/product/HKS009-HCB-ENG.

21   Bates & Rosenbloom (1998) page 1

Guadalupe Street for 20 years. So, you can imagine when a wizened safety leader from the oil and gas fields of Northern New Mexico introduced himself to me as a *why baby*, I was tickled pink. (They say if you want to make a cowboy look soft, stand him next to an oil field worker). This safety leader wasn't talking about the five *whys*, although, like many of you, he's very familiar with Six Sigma. He had developed a regular practice of questioning assumptions and curiously exploring operational rationale. "Why?" is often asked after a failure, as a back-of-the-envelope causal analysis or, unhelpfully, recrimination of someone's intentions or decision-making. But this effective safety leader used it to help workers re-examine their assumptions in the face of changing operating conditions.

Most, if not all, high-hazard operations have some kind of written operating procedure. It's a key document for our regulators, but not always for our workers. When I worked at Los Alamos, we had many procedures that dated back decades and were over 50 pages long. There was no way that these were actual working documents. Therefore, it was unreasonable to assume that workers followed these procedures faithfully. Yet entombed in these procedures are important assumptions about hazards, operating conditions, tools, equipment, and prerequisite knowledge and skills. These assumptions, like these documents, fail to help workers make good decisions once they are ignored, forgotten, and unquestioned. Asking, "Why do you use that tool?" or, "How are you addressing the energy hazard?" or, "Why do you repeat that step?" keeps workers aware and critical of the decisions they make to execute a procedure safely, or not.

The CIA began developing their anti-Castro program in May of 1960, long before Kennedy took office and even before Eisenhower asked for such a strategy. Each time they presented the plan, first to Eisenhower and then to various groups and officials over several months, they adapted it to address each audience's concerns. This resulted in losing sight of several key assumptions and making the outcomes needed for success less attainable. For example, Kennedy became concerned that the original proposed landing site, the city of Trinidad, was "too spectacular . . . too much like a World War II invasion."[22] However, this site was crucial to key assumptions, including the belief that the risk of a failed landing would be mitigated if the insurgents could disappear into the mountains, join the existing resistance fighters, and rally for an attack from within. The Trinidad site was closely surrounded by mountains, but the new site, the Bay of Pigs, was surrounded by swamps with the mountains eighty miles away. One mistake in critical thinking was not to surface how the Trinidad site supported important assumptions for the success of the plan: "Why did we choose Trinidad?" The other was not to examine the presumed outcomes associated with the Trinidad site against those of the Bay of Pigs site: "What are the options for the insurgents to avoid capture and gather reinforcements if the Bay of Pigs landing doesn't go as planned?" After the landing site changed, the CIA continued to argue that the plan couldn't fail because, if something went wrong, the insurgents could simply "melt into the mountains," despite the fact there were no mountains near the Bay of Pigs. Of the roughly 1,400 men in the brigade that landed at the Bay of Pigs, 114 died in the attack and 1,189 were captured and ransomed. Few, if any, joined the resistance in the mountains.

Address power dynamics and create psychological safety

A reluctance to speak up and voice concerns or contrary opinions can arise from a fear of being perceived unfavorably by others. Power differences

---

22   Bates & Rosenbloom (1998) page 7

are a common source of this fear, particularly in hierarchical systems like the military, government, and political structures. Yet power dynamics aren't always easy to predict. For example, Kennedy asked the joint chiefs of staff, a body of the most senior uniformed leaders in the Department of Defense, to evaluate the CIA's anti-Castro program. This group of highly powerful military experts decided to mute their severe doubts about the CIA's plans because they were concerned it was not their role to undermine an agency. Their lack of criticism and equivocal language sounded like approval to Kennedy, who then authorized preparations for the invasion to continue. Other powerful political officials, including Secretary of State Rusk who feared being seen as "soft" on communism, kept quiet about their concerns or pulled their punches. Although Kennedy actively sought advice and opinions from many quarters, he only received meek responses.

Imagine, like Kennedy, you have taken on a new leadership role in a different organization. You aren't aware of the power dynamics or the communication norms. Should you expect people to come to you if they have a problem (you have an "open-door policy" after all)? No. Should you expect people to be candid about their concerns and be appropriately critical of poor decisions and senseless plans? No, of course not. Always expect that there is some level of interpersonal fear in any organization. Psychological safety can never be assumed and must always be rekindled and fostered in any group interaction.

So, what can you do? First, make sure everyone *feels* included. Yes, many different people and groups were ultimately informed of the anti-Castro program, but many did not feel that their concerns would be wanted, valued, or heard. It's simply not enough to bring different people to the table. A study by Amy Edmondson and Henrik Bresman of 62 teams in the pharmaceutical industry found that those teams that were diverse and had psychological safety were considerably more effective than those that were just diverse. So, tell those you include why you want their perspective and positively reinforce unique, contradictory, and outsider ideas and contributions. That does not mean you have to agree with those different views—just let them know why you are glad they brought it up *and mean it*. Public positive reinforcement of difference is tremendously powerful. It doesn't just help the individual receiving the recognition, but it also signals to the rest of the group that it is safe to show their difference. Before long, you will be saying to someone you thought you figured out ages ago: "I never thought you felt that way. Thanks for telling me; I needed to hear it."

A second important consideration is how you as a leader shape and reinforce roles. Roles play an important part in power dynamics. Just think about how someone's demeanor changes when they put on a uniform. If you want people to feel comfortable challenging assumptions, questioning logic, identifying unintended consequences, or generating diverse alternatives, it's important to help them reconcile those activities with how they perceive their role. Consider the behavior of the joint chief of staff when asked to review the CIA's anti-Castro plan. During the Eisenhower administration, their role was to brief the president rather than advise on policy, so they took that position in their report and limited their opinions. If Kennedy had explicitly asked them to be the devil's advocates and lend a critical eye to the CIA's assumptions from a military perspective, he would have received much more useful information. Create a rotating devil's advocate and outsider perspective roles in your teams. Be clear about what is being asked of those roles, such as, "Look at this plan from the perspective of the regulator and raise the concerns you think they would have." Don't let the same person play the same role consistently, and don't only have one lonely contrarian in a meeting. And again, positively reinforce their divergent thoughts and contributions.

Finally, setting ground rules for expressing disagreement reduces the anxiety of offending someone or being offended. One easy rule is not to use adjectives when evaluating an idea. For example, if you think someone's suggestion is "ridiculous," stop and reflect why you judge it that way, and then speak your *why* instead of your judgment: "Your idea could cost more than we have budgeted for repairs this quarter." Another good rule is not to use the words "never" and "always" because they are, by their nature, exaggerations and tend to come up when emotions are heightened. Similarly, it's helpful to establish that only ideas will be attacked, never people. And finally, set the expectation that no point is ever obvious to everyone. Make the rule that arguments must include assumptions, reasoning, observations, and experiences but must exclude words like "clearly" and "obviously." Set ground rules that address the critical thinking blind spots of your organizational culture. Maybe your culture is confrontational and "might makes right," so less assertive voices are rarely heard. In that case, you might set the expectation that everyone will speak, and set a time limit. Or maybe your culture is *too nice*. In that case, set the expectation that everyone is needed to stress-test ideas and decisions, so critical feedback is a gift of improvement. Setting healthy boundaries around critical communication will reduce social anxiety, improve participation, and increase learning and creativity.

Stop solution-finding and start problem-solving

Many leaders feel a strong pressure to solve issues fast—even more so when the problem is high-risk. But of course, that's the wrong instinct. Yes, there are several ways to problem solve and make good decisions quickly. Those processes have clearly defined roles, open channels of communication, and explicit rules for evaluating the quality of the decision. Without such a structure, leaders who feel the pressure to fix things tend to rely on simplicity and "common sense" to go fast. But remember, difficult problems are usually novel and complex. "Common sense" is just another term for force-fitting your current situation into your existing knowledge. If a problem is truly difficult, if it arose from a novel situation, if it intersects multiple relationships between people, processes, and policies, that's not going to work. You're going to have to think critically and do differently.

A study on workplace discrimination suggests that the pressure to quickly make decisions leads to unethical behavior.[23] Taking time to assess alternatives also improves risk identification and mitigation. The ethic of "move fast and break things" attributed to Meta's Mark Zuckerberg assumes the immense resources needed to produce multiple iterations of something until you happen upon something that works. But this approach doesn't take time to challenge assumptions and learn fully from previous failures, so people are more likely to test multiple things with superficial differences rather than fundamental improvements. So, the question becomes where you want to invest. Do you want to invest time and effort into robustly defining the problem, identifying multiple solution options, challenging the assumptions of each option, integrating solution ideas, and testing your ideas in different conditions, or would you rather put your resources into attempting to recover from the blind spots and

---

23   Dana Kanze, Mark A. Conley, and E. Tory Higgins. The motivation of mission statements: How regulatory mode influences workplace discrimination." Organizational Behavior and Human Decision Processes 166 (2021): 84-103, https://www.sciencedirect.com/science/article/pii/S0749597818301092?via%3Dihub

failures of a hasty decision? I mean, after all, you could get lucky. But I don't know many safety leaders who are also gamblers.

How does critical thinking create safety capacity?

I mentioned in the previous chapter that Todd Conklin's blue line is really a series of learning curves. The workers are adapting to changes in work conditions by making decisions, trying out solutions, and learning from what happens. Operationally, the quality of those decisions is the difference between crashing into the red (hazard) line, avoiding it, or moving far away from it. Building critical thinking—such as questioning assumptions, engaging different points of view, producing multiple alternatives, and considering potential consequences, variable conditions, and changing circumstances—into operational touch points will help workers forge the most effective and safe blue line.

At the organizational level, critical thinking will help leaders better identify and address system weaknesses. Seeking out information and perspectives at all levels of the organization, especially from those close to the work, is vital to system improvement. Getting the information leaders need requires creating a psychologically safe environment, which builds learning and problem-solving capacity at the psychological level. Furthermore, critical thinking when making administrative changes will prevent inadvertently creating organizational-level hazards. And better organizational decisions rely on trust and honest communication between groups—which again build the psychological capacity to address safety concerns at both the organizational and operational levels.

Build critical thinking into your regular leadership practice

After the Bay of Pigs failure, President Kennedy did indeed learn a valuable lesson. He realized that the CIA and other groups involved in the program fell into the trap of solution selling, and he in turn tried to force fit the proposed solution to meet the global political challenges he was facing. He and his administration did not engage in effective critical thinking. His brother Robert led the effort to improve decision-making in the executive branch. This required structuring critical thinking practices into the roles, responsibilities, communication, and execution of the Oval Office. Improving critical thinking in your organization and operations also entails some discipline.

<u>Robustly define the problem</u>. Building on the practice of questioning discussed in the previous chapter, the first step toward critically approaching a decision is defining the problem and identifying the assumptions underlying potential solutions. In most cases, the problems won't be expressed as a true problem statement but as a solution; for example, "We need to retrain everybody on lockout/tagout because we are having increased violations." To better understand problems in social systems (all organizations, teams, and work crews are social systems), I like to use the CHIP model based on organizational change theory. CHIP stands for Consequences, Habits, Identity, and Power. Asking questions about these four aspects of the problem provides you with the motivational context in which people are acting. This will help uncover why people are acting as they are and what hidden systemic influences are at play.

	Using the lockout/tagout example, here are some lines of inquiry you might take to "CHIP" away at the problem.
Consequences	What are the realized and potential negative consequences of these violations? Discuss the safety consequences as well as the administrative, operational, and regulatory ones. What about the consequences on morale, interpersonal tension, or other psychological outcomes? Are there positive consequences? Do workers get any benefit from not following the procedure? For example, someone might leave the key in the lock out of concern that they might lose it. In what ways might leaders or the organization get some direct or indirect benefit from this? For example, a more experienced worker might delegate the lockout/tagout for their task to a less experienced person while they do another task that is more difficult.
Habits	Inquire about normal work and ask about the common habits and norms. For example, if it's a quick job where the worker doesn't expect to step away, do they just shut down the equipment controls and not bother to use a lock? What other habits have workers, supervisors, leaders, safety personnel, and others formed around the procedure? Where are the locks kept? How is the procedure supervised? What is ignored and what is noticed?
Identity	This line of inquiry focuses on how the people involved see themselves and their respective roles. In the lockout/tagout example, you might inquire about the different attitudes and habits of the more experienced workers versus the rookies. Or could there be a difference between people associated with one crew versus another crew? Could different job titles see the procedure differently or see it as only relevant to a specific role but not theirs? Or could certain groups, such as contractors, be perceived as outsiders and therefore not supervised the same way or included in safety briefings on the topic?

Power	Asking questions in this vein helps you uncover influences not addressed in previous questions. Consider all the forces that influence work. Maybe there was a companywide earnings call where the CEO emphasized how important efficiency is to making margins. A statement like, "We need to cut out unnecessary steps," may have influenced workers to skip some of the more tedious steps in the lockout/tagout procedure. I once heard a story about how the power of social media influenced workers to take risks that they wouldn't under other circumstances. These workers were trying to bring services back to a neighborhood, and residents came out and started recording them with their phones. The fear of being doxed online influenced them to take unnecessary risks. Power shows up in many unexpected quarters. For example, an influential foreman has developed a rivalry with another foreman and has created an atmosphere of unhealthy competition. Questions about power might start by asking, "Who's the most powerful or respected person in the crew, team, or group?" followed up with, "What are some things people do to stay in their good graces?" Ask about rivalries, pressure they feel, and feared retribution from these powerful people and groups.

Integrate critical thinking techniques into problem-solving processes. Once you have a robust understanding of the problem, *enlist diverse perspectives* to *brainstorm multiple alternatives.* If you don't have an opportunity to bring different stakeholders into the room, assign people to represent the interests of different stakeholders, such as customers, leaders, and other groups that provide inputs into and use the outputs of your work. Once you have an extensive list of options, uncover and *challenge the assumptions* of those options. For example, a solution might assume that all workers on the site, even contractors, have the same lockout/tagout training, or that all workers fluently speak the same language. Consider and discuss how the solution might change if the assumption was not true, or if the opposite of the assumption was true. Another way to challenge the assumptions underneath a solution is to consider how the solution would work in *different contexts*. One solution might be effective when the energized system is inside a building, but not when working on a system outdoors. *Assigning devil's advocates* is another method for challenging assumptions and solutions. Clients I work with like to rotate their devil's advocate assignments so challenges come from different perspectives and people are less inclined to stop listening to the naysayer. In less psychologically safe environments, it's always a good idea to assign two or more devil's advocates, because there is

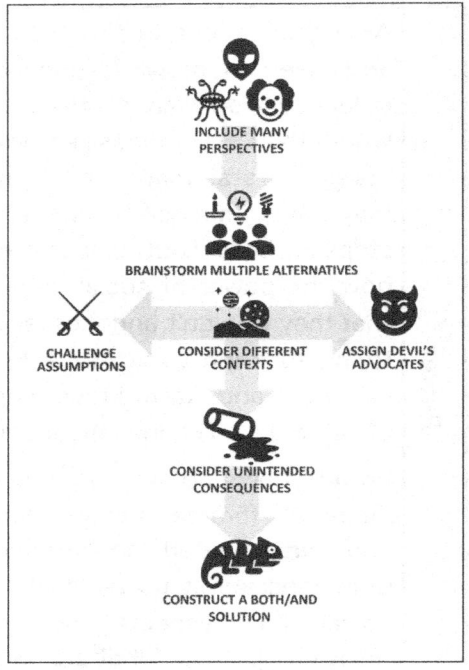

Figure 3: Critical Thinking Process

power in numbers. Once you have whittled down a few options, consider the unintended consequences of each solution. Take the best aspects of multiple solutions *to construct a both/and solution* that addresses multiple risks and concerns. Avoid getting into a contest of solutions where people advocate one idea over another and ignore the best aspects of each.

Critical Thinking Reflection Questions

1. Reflect on a regular but important operation or task your team does. Can you list a few of the assumptions underlying that task? What if those assumptions were no longer true? What if the opposite of those assumptions was true? What changes can you foresee that might undermine those assumptions?

2. What is the worst thing that your team could fail to tell you? What are all the reasons someone might want to withhold that from you? Consider the consequences they might fear, the habits of your team, the identity of the people who have that information, or the power dynamics that might be at play. Are you sure those issues don't exist now? What can you do to address them?

3. Do you feel pressure to solve the problems your team brings to you? Have you ever thought: "It would be so much faster if I just fixed this?" If so, how can you engage others better in problem-solving? How can you enlist your team in critically assessing your solutions and generating alternative solutions?

4. Think of a problem you needed to solve that required the input of several others. How did you feel about getting different perspectives and opinions? How well did you include them in the problem-solving

process? What worked well and what didn't? What might you do differently next time?

5. Consider a decision you or your organization made that had unintended consequences (either positive or negative ones). Why did those consequences come about? Were they foreseeable when the decision was made or the action taken? What steps could have been taken to better assess and prepare for the consequences?

CHAPTER 6: EXPERIMENT

In an uncertain world, isn't every decision you make just an experiment with different confidence intervals?

EXPERIMENT

On April 20, 2023, SpaceX's Starship launched for the first time and after about four minutes experienced a *rapid, unplanned disassembly*. Everyone cheered. Later, Space X tweeted, "With a test like this, success comes from what we learn, and today's test will help us improve Starship's reliability as SpaceX seeks to make life multi-planetary."[24] I'm all for learning from failure, but when I heard the story, I thought: "That's great, but who's going to clean that up?" It struck me as an expensive experiment, not only in terms of the cost of the rocket, but also the environmental impact. When I discuss experimenting with leaders, the pushback I get is based on the same discomfort I had with the SpaceX explosion—"Who has the time and resources for that?"

Experimentation is simply a learning technique for increasing certainty

It can be as simple a task as collecting and confirming information, exploring the nature of your environment or a specific phenomenon, or both. Scientific experiments are highly rigorous (you may be engaged in that kind of work) and require more time and resources than makes sense for most business and operational problems. But that's not what I'm suggesting you do. Instead, I'd like you to consider how to take the principles of the experimental technique and apply them to more common operations. Also, I'm not promoting a *move-fast-and-break-things* approach to learning, which I suspect is part of SpaceX's ethos given its Silicon Valley origins, because it can be a wasteful and dangerous way to learn that unnecessarily gobbles up your capacity for safety and innovation. As I argued in the previous chapter, that approach lacks the critical thinking and rigor required in high-hazard and high-reliability

---

24   Rachel Treisman, "Why SpaceX Staff Cheered When the Starship Rocket Exploded," NPR, (April 2023), https://www.npr.org/2023/04/21/1171202753/spacex-starship-launch-explosion-cheer-success.

environments. However, if your organization faces any uncertainty, and if making a mistake has high consequences, then experimentation is essential. If you have a clear intent on what you need to know, the experiment will be efficient and effective.

In 2002, when discussing Iraq in a press conference, Donald Rumsfeld famously invoked the Johari Window analysis developed by Joseph Luft and Harrington Ingram and used by intelligence professionals to navigate uncertainty. In situations where there is certainty and stability, you are in the quadrant of Known Knowns. In a safety context, we can think of this as times when the black line and blue line are aligned. But if information becomes unclear or unreliable in a stable environment that is somewhat predictable, then you have moved into a situation with *known unknowns*. In other words,

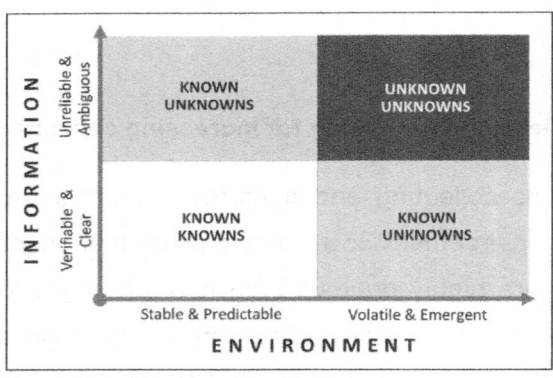

Figure 4: VUCA Johari Window

you know the information you have is wrong because it doesn't jive with the context in which it is being presented, so you need to find the correct information. Likewise, you might be in an emergent and changeable situation, but you feel confident that the information you are getting is correct, so your objective is to use that information to find some pattern in the chaotic situation. In this case, the *known unknowns* arise from a lack of predictability in the environment. An example of *known unknowns* is a warning indicator going off in a cockpit. If there are blue skies and everything seems to be going smoothly on the flight, then the question you might ask yourself is, "What's going wrong with the gauge to give me bad information?" But if you are flying through a storm, you might think: "What is this gauge telling me that will help me better understand the nature of this weather?" In both scenarios you can increase certainty with structured inquiry. In the blue-skies scenario, you would look at other indicators to see if they corroborate or contradict the one that appears to be faulty. In the stormy scenario, you would change your environment or make some other compensation, perhaps ascend above the storm, and check if the indicator changes accordingly.

If you happen to be in a VUCA situation,[25] one which is volatile, uncertain, complex, and ambiguous, you can rely on neither good information nor a stable environment. Here, your only option for learning and navigating the situation is to experiment. Because you are in the realm of *unknown unknowns*, all you can do is make your best guess, based on reason and past experience, about what might happen if you were to do something. If reason and experience lead you astray, no matter. When you don't know what you don't know, figuring out what's wrong is almost as valuable as discerning what's right. In fact, guessing the right answer on a pop quiz is less effective for learning than getting the wrong answer, because we tend to be much more curious about why we are wrong than why we unknowingly were right. The most important thing about your best guess is the *why* behind the effect you expect to produce if you do something. This is what you are testing when you either get the result you expected or not.

---

25 VUCA is a term attributed to the US Army War College, which used it in the late 1980s to describe the global political climate after the Cold War. It's often used in management literature to describe the increasingly complex global business climate.

An experiment begins with a hypothesis

A hypothesis is a tentative explanation for an observation, phenomenon, or problem that can be tested. Furthermore, a hypothesis explains the relationships between variables that are explicit and measurable or observable. The three types of relationships most commonly tested with experiments are correlation, prediction, and causation. A hypothesis about correlation is, "In November, December, and January, slips and falls will increase." You know that a change in the date doesn't directly cause people to slip and fall, but investigating this hypothesis will help you identify a shared factor between the two variables, such as icy weather, which can help you identify controls such as gritting sidewalks.

Prediction is understanding how the value of an independent variable might predict the value of an independent variable. A predictive hypothesis is, "If an El Niño weather pattern forms in the Pacific, then there will be an increased risk of forest fires in the Rockies." Again, El Niño isn't posited as a direct cause of forest fires, but statistical analysis might show that this weather pattern in one part of the country is a good predictor of a phenomenon in another, enabling forest management and emergency services to prepare accordingly.

A causal relationship is when a dependent variable changes as a direct result of a change in an independent variable. In social science, true causal experiments don't happen—leadership and safety practices fall squarely in the realm of social science. However, although it's difficult, if not impossible, to *prove* causation, many of the decisions we make as leaders are based on causal hypotheses: "If I do this, then this will happen." Take for example Zuckerberg San Francisco General Hospital (ZSFG), which tried to improve patient outcomes in its emergency department by lowering patients' length of stay (LOS).[26] Their hypothesis was, "If we replace one-way-communication pagers with a two-way-communication messaging app for orthopedic and neurological patients who need a specialist consultation, then length of stay for these patients will decrease." Remember, the underlying *why* of a hypothesis is important. In this case, the hospital believed that outdated pager communication, which required specialist residents to make a phone call to get the information they needed, was much less efficient than two-way text communication, which included the ability to share media between the emergency doctors and the specialist doctors. If ZSFG could show and quantify the benefits of the two-way communication app, then they could justify an investment in changing their communication processes to improve patient outcomes.

An experiment is limited and controlled

When ZSFG decided to test whether they could improve patient outcomes by introducing two-way communication to the specialist consult process, they didn't roll the messaging app out to the entire hospital, they devised a pilot. Only select teams in orthopedics and neurology would switch from using pagers to using the app for a specific period of time. This is important because we always have a bias toward upholding our hypothesis—it is our *best* guess, after all. The truth is that every decision we make is an experiment; only the confidence intervals vary. When we are in the realm of known knowns, our confidence can be high that our best guess about the outcome of a decision or action will be true most of the time. But when working in a VUCA environment, where there are unknown unknowns, we

---

26 M.J. Kerrissey & M. Kuznetsova, "Killing the Pager at ZSFG," Harvard Business Publishing: Harvard T.H. Chan School of Public Health, (2022), https://caseresources.hsph.harvard.edu/publications/killing-pager-zsfg.

can't give in to the pressure to quickly solve problems. Implementing your best guess in this environment could result in unforeseen consequences. Consider the Cybertruck recall in April of 2024.[27] Workers found a solution to getting the pedal pad placed properly on the pedal—dish soap. Unfortunately, drivers found that traces of the slippery soap allowed the pad to come off and trap the accelerator pedal down. According to the National Highway Transportation Safety Administration, this solution wasn't approved and therefore one can assume wasn't tested. The soap "solution" was an uncontrolled experiment on 3,878 pricey vehicles.

In an experiment, failure is expected and mitigated

Admittedly, ZSFG was hopeful that the new messaging app they were testing would outperform pagers and improve LOS. But if it didn't, doctors were not barred from using pagers, and the analysis of the results of the experiment factored in app usage. In fact, the experiment failed to support ZSFG's hypothesis. Although there were anecdotes about the new messaging app's effectiveness, the final numbers showed no significant improvement in LOS. Nevertheless, ZSFG learned something unexpected about the nature of communication between emergency department physicians and specialist residents that would inform future efforts to improve efficiency. Emergency doctors loved the ease of communication with the app and started using it for much more than requesting consults. They asked *quick questions* and provided patient follow-up information. Specialist residents, who worked long shifts and whose workload

---

[27] Camila Domonoske, "Tesla Recalls Cybertruck Over Sticky Problem. Blame It on — Yes — Soap," NPR (April 2024), https://www.npr.org/2024/04/19/1245849907/tesla-cybertruck-recall-accelerator-soap.

required that they prioritize emergency consults and other activities that necessitated specialist care, had difficulty sorting through all the non-emergency communications. The benefit of the pagers was that they required as much time commitment on the part of the emergency staff as they did of the specialist residents. The emergency department would page their phone number and wait for the specialist to call back to explain what they needed, so they kept their communications to only what was necessary. The specialists were conditioned to respond quickly to the page because the only way to know if the call was important was to actually speak to the emergency department staff. Any communications technology the emergency department might use going forward would need a way to flag urgency and avoid distracting specialists with non-urgent communications when they were working on a high-priority case.

How does experimentation create safety capacity?

As I mentioned earlier, experimentation is the only way to create knowledge in a VUCA environment where there are unknown unknowns. As safety professionals, you recognize that the greatest hazard is the one you don't know about. All organizations, especially in the face of volatility and ambiguity, experience strong strategic pressure to do something to improve performance and respond to change. Research suggests that a drive for expediency, which creates the corporate messages that bias action over learning, tends to encourage unethical behavior.[28] When faced with both uncertainty and expediency, it makes sense that we cheat, discriminate, and otherwise try to increase our chances of "winning"

---

28 Dana Kanze et al., "The Motivation of Mission Statements: How Regulatory Mode Influences Workplace Discrimination," ScienceDirect, https://www.sciencedirect.com/science/article/pii/S0749597818301092?via%3Dihub.

in a difficult and urgent situation. That, of course, is the wrong instinct when it comes to safety because it reduces trust, encourages shortcuts, discourages candid conversation, and in other ways greatly reduces safety capacity. Experimentation is a better approach to innovating in the face of uncertainty.

I have heard from many of my colleagues that an impediment to a thriving ongoing practice of learning teams—a proven technique for building safety capacity into operations—is the frustration workers feel when they can't get the management buy-in and resources needed to implement more sophisticated engineered safety controls. Experimenting, specifically prototyping and piloting, can help workers build the business case for safety innovations. The discipline of creating a hypothesis and identifying measurable and/or observable variables clarifies for decision-makers the risk and reward of a proposal, while small-scale prototypes and pilots are easier to fund and approve. No one wants to make a big investment in an uncertain outcome (except maybe Space X), so building a practice of experimentation is an investment toward efficiency and effectiveness.

At the psychological level, experimentation can build greater comfort in uncertainty and a healthy relationship to failure. One way to build psychological safety is by setting boundaries, and the disciplined approach of experimentation takes a measured bite out of the VUCA elephant. Likewise, preparing for and even anticipating the insights from failure in an experiment reduces our natural fear of failure and promotes a healthy curiosity that builds safety capacity, as argued in chapter 4.

Integrate experimentation into your regular leadership practice

Experimentation provides a structured way of addressing uncertainty, reducing bias, and discovering more about the error-prone situations and the systemic safety traps your workers are navigating. Bringing experimentation into your leadership practice does not require organizing, building, and executing large, complex experiments. You don't even need to use a statistical package—the simple data analysis and visualizations built into spreadsheet software is sufficient. In fact, you don't need to conduct an experiment at all. Albert Einstein's most celebrated discoveries were the outcomes of thought experiments.

<u>State your hypotheses explicitly</u>. This alone is a powerful way to manage uncertainty and develop a better understanding in situations when information is unreliable and the environment is unstable. When making a consequential decision, or when implementing a solution under uncertainty, take a moment to formulate the hypothesis underlying it: "If I do this, then I expect that to happen." Identify the variables you expect to affect and determine the relationship you hypothesize them to have. Consider the example a colleague recently shared with me. While investigating an incident of administering a non-injurious overdose of medication to a child, a hospital found that many of their scales in treatment rooms measured imperial pounds, while their dosage calculation system used kilograms to determine how much medication to administer. This meant, in many but not all cases, providers had to convert pounds to kilograms before inputting that parameter, creating an error-prone situation. Let's imagine that the safety team at this hospital decided to run an experiment. Although it seems obvious that changing all the scales in treatment rooms to display kilograms instead of pounds would solve the problem, it is unclear how often this mistake has been made, and the cost to the hospital to make this change is not insignificant. A competing solution, offered by the tech team, is to add a pop-up to the software reminding providers to make the conversion if needed. The safety team's hypothesis is therefore, "Using scales in kilograms to weigh patients will

reduce weight input mistakes more than seeing a pop-up reminder to check if weight measures need to be converted."

Identify variables and plan how to measure or observe them. This hypothesis identifies an independent variable and a dependent one. The use of an error reduction intervention is the independent variable, and it has three values: (1) use of scales, (2) use of a pop-up reminder, or (3) no intervention. This independent variable allows the team to compare two interventions and includes a control where the value of the variable is zero. The dependent variable is the number of weight input mistakes. Note that the dependent variable isn't dosage mistakes, because the team wants to control for mistakes that aren't related to the issues with converting pounds to kilograms. The beauty of this hypothesis is that there is only one independent variable—don't overwhelm yourself with too many indicators. But the challenge is how to measure it. In the anecdote, the provider self-reported the mistake. This is an unreliable data -collection strategy. If there is no automatic way to identify mistakes, then the team will need to pull the data from the experiment and analyze it to find weights in the dosage calculation that do not align with the weight in the patient's chart or within range for a child of that age. It's very important that you choose an independent variable that can be reliably measured or observed.

Conduct pilots or experiments on samples of your populations to test your hypothesis. Because the hospital has three values for the independent variable, or intervention, the safety team must create three groups: one that gets the first intervention, one that gets the second, and a control group that doesn't get an intervention at all. A key consideration for the size of the group is how you will analyze the data. If you have the capability to do statistical analysis, choose the size of the group based on the sample size needed for statistical validity. However, for learning purposes, a simple frequency analysis (calculating mistake frequency per patient volume on average) is sufficient if you carefully consider other factors a statistical analysis can otherwise adjust for. Some practical factors the hospital will need to consider are how many kilogram scales they can get their hands on and how to assemble a large enough sample to show an effect even if mistakes are infrequent. If just doing a simple frequency analysis, they will need to ensure the three groups are roughly the same size, so as not to amplify the effect in a larger group. Finally, the hospital team must consider how long they will collect data. If mistakes are infrequent, the team will need to run the experiment longer.

<u>Plan for failure</u>. Be open to the possibility of being surprised by the results. Also consider unintended consequences of the interventions and create controls for them. In the hospital example, the safety team will want to monitor results and get feedback from participants throughout the experiment just in case, for example, the pop-up has an unwanted effect on using the dosing calculator, or the kilogram scales have a deleterious effect on other processes that use weight as an important input. Be prepared to stop the experiment if your interventions are doing harm.

<u>Conduct thought experiments</u>. Although I am describing a somewhat involved experiment with the hospital example, you can bring experimentation into your leadership practice with little investment by conducting thought experiments. Examples of famous thought experiments are Einstein's train and embankment thought experiment, Schrödinger's cat, Zeno's paradoxes, and the infinite monkey theorem. The steps are essentially the same. Begin with a hypothesis that clearly defines the variables of your experiment and the relationship you posit between those variables. Think about how you would measure or observe those variables and design the experiment. Consider the different ways the hypothesis might be disproven. For example, think about how your

experiment would work under different conditions, with different people, and when there is misinformation, misunderstanding, or changes. You might also construct a thought experiment on a hypothesis that is the opposite of what you believe to be true. In your mind, construct an experiment and create conditions under which your *anti-hypothesis* might prove true.

The most important thing to remember when bringing experimentation into your leadership practice is that it is your best tool for learning in VUCA environments. Don't be afraid of making decisions or taking action under uncertainty. Just recognize that you are operating from a hypothesis that can either be true or false. Either way, be curious about why and consider what that might mean about related factors you don't yet understand. Basically, the mindset of experimentation that safety leaders must cultivate to build safety capacity can be expressed in the mantra, "I seek to understand the relationship between actions and outcomes and what that teaches us about the environment in which we do consequential work."

Experimentation Reflection Questions

1. Reflect on what is volatile, uncertain, complex, and ambiguous in your current environment. What are the most consequential decisions you need to make in this environment? Are there opportunities for experimentation to improve your understanding and make better decisions?

2. Think about the normal work your team does. Is it safe to assume that they are operating in the realm of *known knowns*? If not, what are the *known unknowns*? What potential unknown unknowns concern you the most?

3. What is one important action you plan to take this week? Write down a key hypothesis that informs that action. What are the variables in your hypothesis? What's the relationship between them? How might you measure or observe them? What's a simple way to test if your hypothesis is true?

4. Identify one important safety control you use in your operations. What is a primary hypothesis that informs its function? (For example, for fall protection the hypothesis might be, "If a person falls from a height, wearing a body harness attached to anchored cable, it will arrest the fall.") Next, conduct a thought experiment that would disprove that hypothesis. Consider the conditions under which the hypothesis is no longer true. Identify variables for those conditions and how those variables might be measured or observed. Based on the failure parameters of the control, hypothesize a more robust control. How would you test its robustness?

CHAPTER 7: DEVELOP EMOTIONAL RESILIENCY

If emotions shape our perceptions and motivate our actions, isn't leadership an emotional practice?

He called everyone "cowboys and buttheads."[29] Vice admiral Pete Nanos's apoplectic outbursts were epic. He was appointed to lead Los Alamos National Laboratory, the storied birthplace of the atomic bomb, by President George W. Bush to *drain the swamp* of a perceived culture of indifference to safety and security at the Laboratory. This reputation was reinforced in the eyes of the media and regulators with a Chinese espionage scare, missing classified disks, and safety violations that all proved, after investigations and prosecutions, to be less egregious than portrayed. I was the training team leader for Nuclear Materials Technology at the time of Nanos's reign. Certainly, there were major safety and security concerns that kept me and my team buried under corrective actions, but the root of the issue was weakness in organizational and operational capacity exacerbated by a deteriorating physical plant. Pete Nanos didn't see it that way.

Sometime in 2004, a vehicle was parked at Technical Area 3 with a bumper sticker simply declaring "Work-Free Safe Zone." Nanos called an all-hands meeting where he vented his anger at the scientists' *culture of arrogance* and famously referred to laboratory employees as "cowboys and buttheads." In July of 2004, additional classified disks were thought to be missing, and a student was injured by a laser beam. Nanos issued a memo that said: "I don't care how many people I have to fire to make it stop. If you think the rules are silly, if you think compliance is a joke, please resign now and save me the trouble." Then he shut down the laboratory. My team and I were among the few permitted to do work because we were tasked with implementing the corrective actions to restart the nuclear

---

29 Hugh Gusterson, "The Assault on Los Alamos National Laboratory: A Drama in Three Acts," SageJournals, (November 2011), https://journals.sagepub.com/doi/full/10.1177/0096340211426631.

facilities. Other employees experienced the daily irony of coming to work with the explicit imperative of not doing any work while there—for seven months. The shutdown cost taxpayers an estimated $370 million and led to the furlough of thousands of workers at both Los Alamos and Livermore National Laboratories. The bumper sticker was right.

This is the origin story of the HOP (Human and Organizational Performance) movement in safety. Todd Conkin was my boss at the time. He and other leaders in our division pulled together experts from inside and outside the Laboratory to grapple with systemic issues that plagued the National Laboratories and dispel the myths surrounding human error. Draft zero of what became Todd's *Principles of Human Performance* was debated over green chile breakfast burritos. And the catalyst of all this was one *really angry dude*.

Emotions play a fundamental role in all social systems

Emotions are pre-cognitive, which means they affect the way we perceive things, make decisions, and act, often without our conscious knowledge. In fact, neurological studies have shown that a lack of emotions does not help us be more rational; instead, when our emotional functioning is impaired, so is our decision-making. Both pleasurable and painful emotions play a fundamental role in how humans operate at work. Emotions tell us what is important and make our work meaningful. Pleasurable emotions increase creativity, help us integrate ideas, and improve inductive reasoning. Painful emotions improve our attention to detail, help us uncover errors, and thus drive better information processing and problem-solving. Both pleasurable and painful emotions are conduits to building bonds with others and help us navigate complex social interactions. Emotions are the basis of intuition, they are the conveyers of our deep learning and expertise, and they are the reason we can think fast on our feet.

Emotions also create biases. For example, strong emotions, both painful and pleasurable, can provoke a costly bias called *escalation of commitment*, commonly known as throwing good money after bad. Other biases of emotional tagging include self-interest bias, confirmation bias, and groupthink—all of which can lead to disastrous decisions. Emotions have other ways of derailing work. You have probably heard of *amygdala hijack*, where fear, originating from our limbic system, drives us to fight, flee, freeze, or flatter. Organizations that are perceived as dangerous, perhaps because they are rife with blame or unhealthy competition, tend to have decreased communication, collaboration, and work effort while experiencing increased absenteeism and politics. Pete Nanos's unrestrained anger, the bias it erected against Laboratory employees, and the fear it instilled in everyday operations and interactions had disastrous consequences. That was the first time I had been exposed to James Reason's *blame cycle*—as I read the description of the phenomenon, I recognized the very fabric of the culture Nanos had created.

Awareness and acceptance of emotions

The key to harnessing emotions for positive outcomes (and avoiding bad outcomes) is awareness and acceptance of emotions. Self-awareness and social awareness are the foundational skills of emotional intelligence. As I said before, emotions are pre-cognitive, but just because they arise outside our awareness does not mean we can't turn our attention to them. In his many books and articles, Daniel Goleman cites research that suggests emotional intelligence to be the most important set of skills for leaders to develop. Emotional intelligence has an outsized influence on the performance of individuals and teams,[30] with studies suggesting that even in engineering fields, emotional intelligence is more important to effectiveness on the job than technical skill.[31] When we recognize and accept the emotions we and others feel, we are better able to motivate ourselves and others, we have a more realistic assessment of ourselves and expectations of others, we can be more authentic and gain the trust of others, and we are more open to change, more optimistic, and better able to persuade others.[32]

Let's consider how things could have been different for Vice Admiral Nanos if he had better emotional awareness. It was certainly understandable for him to be angry. A security breach of classified nuclear weapons information not only put the country at risk, but potentially risked the lives of the service people he previously led and cared for. Lapses in safety in a nuclear facility are equally serious, not only risking the life and health of employees but of the community. Anger is an emotion that moves us to action despite personal risk—whistleblowers report that anger and other intense emotions motivated them to risk their careers and report wrongdoing.[33] But unexamined anger can also reinforce bias, like what Nanos held against "arrogant scientists," and drive blame of others as

---

30   Ernest H. O'Boyle Jr. et al., "The Relation Between Emotional Intelligence and Job Performance: A Meta-Analysis," *Journal of Organizational Behavior*, (June 2011), https://onlinelibrary.wiley.com/doi/abs/10.1002/job.714.

31   Richard Boyatzis, "Emotional Intelligence Competencies in Engineer's Effectiveness and Engagement," Emerald Insight, (February 2017), https://www.emerald.com/insight/content/doi/10.1108/CDI-08-2016-0136/full/html.

32   Daniel Goleman, "What Makes a Leader?" Harvard Business Review, (January 2004), https://hbr.org/2004/01/what-makes-a-leader.

33   Erika Henik, "Mad as Hell or Scared Stiff? The Effects of Value Conflict and Emotions on Potential Whistle-Blowers." J Bus Ethics 80, 111–119 (2008). doi.org/10.1007/s10551-007-9441, https://link.springer.com/article/10.1007/s10551-007-9441-1.

an ego defense against fear of recrimination. If Nanos had paused to recognize his anger, then accepted his anger as a reasonable emotional response in this situation, then he could have used the seriousness his anger was signaling to take effective action. Serious consideration of the situation, along with his extensive experience as a leader, would have led him to be curious about the problem and its potential solutions, rather than rashly moving to punishment and humiliation. And even if the heat of his anger couldn't be contained before it reached others, awareness of their emotional reactions would have afforded another opportunity for recovery.

Have you ever blown your top and once the steam cleared, looked around you at the shocked faces and defensive body language of those around you? What did you do? Blame your emotions on them? Pretend nothing happened? I wouldn't recommend either of those responses, although they are normal ego defenses. Acceptance of the situation, in other words, recognizing it for what it is and not trying to shield yourself from that reality, brings the humility needed to address it: "I'm sorry for my outburst. I can see it has made you all uncomfortable, and that wasn't my intention. If you will forgive me and allow me another chance to explain calmly what's bothering me, maybe we can find a path forward together." Awareness and acceptance (note that acceptance is absolutely not the same as approval) are the thresholds to empathy, trust, collaboration, and problem-solving.

Empathy underlies trust, facilitates collaboration, and improves problem-solving

Even if you recognize that someone is good at what they do, and that they are not misrepresenting themselves, can you really trust them if they have given no thought or consideration to your perspective, feelings, or needs?

There are three kinds of empathy: *cognitive empathy*, or being able to recognize someone else's perspective; *emotional empathy*, or being able to appreciate what someone else feels; and *empathetic concern*, or sensing what someone needs. Just as acceptance is not approval, empathy is not the same as agreement. Recognizing someone else's perspective, feelings, or needs does not mean you think, feel, or desire the same things. In fact, the ability to consider external ideas, emotions, and desires that you yourself do not have is essential to creativity, cooperation, compassion, and other complex social skills.

Imagine if Vice Admiral Nanos had adopted empathy as a way to find a better solution to the Laboratory's safety and security challenges. Once he recognized the fear and defensiveness that his angry outburst provoked and then disarmed the situation with humility, he might have harnessed his curiosity to begin to understand the different perspectives of Laboratory employees. He might have learned, for example, how frustrated employees were with the outdated floppy disk procedure for securing classified material, which forced people to estimate and record how many disks the data would require before it was transferred. This created an error trap in which the number of disks accounted for might not equal the number created. This meant that the "lost" classified disks may have never existed, and worse yet, there might be lost disks that were never accounted for. If he were open and vulnerable about his own confusion about the complex funding system for the Laboratory, employees might have opened up about their fear of spending overhead dollars on modernization efforts such as moving to the more efficient and secure digital system for classified material that Lawrence Livermore National Laboratory was already using. And if he had mustered the compassion to recognize the needs of his employees, he might have seen that after operating for over 60 years as a hybrid scientific, military, manufacturing, and academic institution, the organizational systems had become unnavigable—and needed to be redesigned with a clear shared purpose in mind.

How does emotional resiliency create safety capacity?

Emotional resiliency is the leadership skill that fosters the benefits of emotions for individual and organizational performance while mitigating the destructive potential of emotions. By appropriately responding to emotions as they arise and engaging emotions for learning and improvement, emotional resiliency builds organizational, operational, and psychological resiliency. Consider all the leadership practices I have covered so far—emotional resilience plays a role in all of them. A shared purpose helps align diverging and differing interests at the organizational, operational, and psychological level. Empathy is a necessary skill for uncovering a shared purpose, especially when those involved have different perspectives and needs. It's hard to build a network of genuine relationships that will come to your aid to address a safety issue if you haven't built trust. Openness and curiosity, which spur the inquiry needed to build safety capacity at all levels of the organization, are emotionally based. To create a psychologically safe environment that fosters openness and curiosity, leaders must be vulnerable and able to manage emotionally difficult situations. Critical thinking involves challenging yourself and others by confronting biases and through vigorous debate. These activities require emotional awareness and regulation to keep healthy conflict from getting heated. Experimenting entails confronting the unknown and engaging with failure, both emotionally fraught endeavors. In fact, everything we do as safety leaders involves emotional management. You are creating an environment where people can safely do dangerous work, but the danger is still present. There is a plethora of pleasurable and painful emotions you must manage (for yourself and others) as you engage in the creative and consequential endeavor of building the capacity for safety around inherently risky operations.

Emotional resiliency is an essential daily leadership practice

As I said earlier, the first step is awareness of emotions. I think you will be surprised, as I continue to be, about how difficult this simple thing can be. For example, I was raised with the unquestioned belief that it was not okay to be angry. I certainly have expressed anger, but I have had a very hard time recognizing when I feel angry. For a long time, my only clue that I was angry was when someone else pointed out that I was yelling—seriously. So, my basic practice for building emotional resiliency is just naming my emotions.

We have basic survival emotions that arise from our limbic system, a part of our nervous system anatomy that we share with other mammals. Different streams of literature use slightly different lists of emotions, but I tend to go with the ones most used in neuropsychology: happy, surprised, afraid, angry, sad, and disgusted. I say they are survival emotions because they all provide important functions for surviving in a social system. Happy emotions motivate us to do things that feel good. Surprise makes us notice something different, prompting and reinforcing learning. Fear responds to danger with fight, flight, freeze, or flatter. Anger motivates us to make big changes, like challenging power structures. Sadness helps us respond to loss by inducing the introspection needed for emotional healing. Disgust keeps our appetites in check so that we, for example, don't eat something rotten despite our

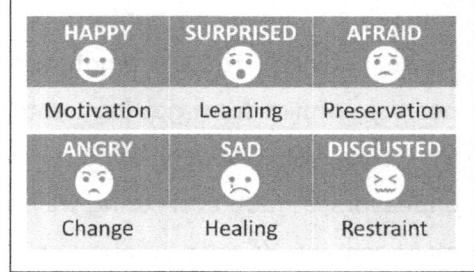

Figure 5: Basic Feelings

hunger. It's an important social teacher. We can register other people's disgust and stay away from something enticing that might harm us without having to sample it.

Develop awareness of your emotions. The first daily leadership practice I suggest is simple: pick one milestone during the day when you will stop and check how you are feeling. By milestone I mean something like when you walk in the door of your office, break for lunch, start a new task, or go into a meeting. Use these small changes in your day as a reminder to pause and scan yourself for an emotion. You likely won't feel a strong emotion, perhaps just a vague mood. But if you check in with your body, you will get a flavor: "My shoulders are a little hunched. I'm feeling a little stressed, which has a tinge of fear in it." Take two seconds to feel the emotion, and then take a big deep breath and continue what you are doing. It's that simple, but not always easy.

Regulate your emotional reactions. Once you get good at noticing how you feel on cue, then start building your awareness of your emotional reactions. Start by reflecting on something that really irks you. It could be a behavior someone does, like showing up late for meetings, or a situation you find yourself in, like not being able to find your ID badge when you need it. Next, let your coyotes howl. By that I mean, be as judgmental as you want about the person doing the annoying behavior, or the situation that makes you crazy, or even yourself. Let yourself rant (in your head) and get all those nasty judgments out (but keep them to yourself). For example, you might judge the person who is always late to meetings as disrespectful, lazy, and entitled. Or perhaps, when you can't find that thing you need, you judge yourself as disorganized and scatterbrained. After your rant, take a deep breath and reflect on your judgments. What feelings do they evoke? When you think of a disrespectful, lazy, and entitled person, are you angry or disgusted? When you think about yourself being

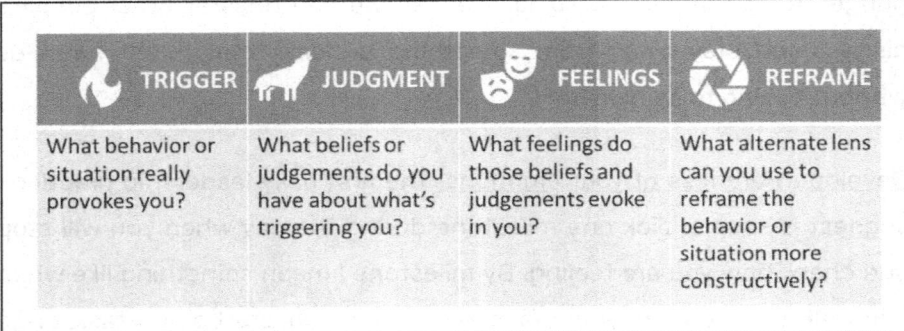

Figure 6: Emotional Agility Process

disorganized and scatterbrained, does it scare you? Now, take a pause. The last step is to explore what frame of mind would help you accept (not approve, just accept) the triggering behavior or situation. Positive psychology provides us with simple ways to reframe the behavior or situation to something less annoying. Professor George Vaillant, in Harvard's longitudinal Study of Adult Development, which began after World War II, identified several attitudes that helped people thrive: patience, courage, humility, gratitude, generosity, forgiveness, humor, and anticipation of a better future. So, for example, imagine that person who is late for a meeting. Instead of letting your coyotes howl, reframe the situation with patience and anticipation. You might think: "Her input into this meeting is important, so we'll wait for her contribution. Afterward, I'll talk to her about why she is needed at the start of the meeting. Then we can come up with a solution." Finally, take another deep breath and check in on how you feel.

Practice empathy. Practices I have already covered involve cognitive empathy, understanding another's perspective. Curiosity opens the door to cognitive empathy, and critical thinking integrates others' perspectives into structured

Constructive Attitudes for Emotional Reframing

Patience	Courage
Humility	Gratitude
Generosity	Forgiveness
Humor	Anticipation
Dignity	Compassion
Respect	Moderation

inquiry. Here, I want explore practices that help you develop your emotional empathy and empathetic concern more fully. Emotional empathy is more helpful than cognitive empathy in understanding people's behavior and attitudes, especially those that seem incomprehensible from a logical lens. Empathetic concern is fundamental to safety leadership because, without it, coaching, feedback, and conflict resolution are largely ineffective.

Let's start with emotional empathy, which, in my experience (strangely enough), is easier than emotional self-awareness, and just as simple. Remember the practice of identifying a shared purpose? The first step was to list several important interactions you have with your team and other stakeholders. From that list, choose your in-person interactions, such as stand-up meetings or pre-job briefs. These will be the milestones in your day, week, or month that will prompt you to check in on others' emotions. For example, in a pre-job brief, once everyone has gathered, take a breath before launching into the agenda, and just feel the vibe in the room. Look around at everyone's expressions and body language, make eye contact, and allow there to be a second or two of silence. Just take mental note of the emotional atmosphere.

One good way to learn more about what others are feeling is just to express your own feelings. When you are making everyday decisions with others, let people know the emotional context you are working in so you can understand theirs: "I'm feeling some trepidation about this solution. It's not because I don't think it's a good idea, but I want to start cautiously. How are you feeling about it?" This simple step of identifying, expressing, and eliciting feelings will go a long way to reducing biases and illuminating blind spots.

If you want to reinforce a positive mood in the room or manage a negative mood, try a positive framing. Start by framing your own thoughts and expressing a positive emotion. For example, if you are starting a process that has had unexpected delays and you are sensing frustration in the room, you could say: "It's taken a while to get here, and I feel grateful to all of you for working to overcome the setbacks. Thank you." You could also just acknowledge the emotions that are present: "I feel a buzz in the room, and it's making me even more excited to kick off this new process." You will be amazed at how much engagement those simple expressions of emotion will garner.

Practicing empathetic concern will not only improve motivation and engagement but also learning and problem-solving. Marshall Rosenberg, who developed the non-violent communication method used by facilitators of contentious diplomatic negotiations, asserts that the best way to engage in a conflict, or any other important communication, is on the basis of needs. For example, if someone stormed into your office demanding a change in your decision or your behavior, instead of confronting the demand, recognize and evaluate the need behind that demand. I'm not talking about their rationale, but what needs a change would fulfill.

One important role our emotions play is to alert us to our needs. Four basic types of needs are as follows:

- *Physical needs*, which include a safe and comfortable work environment, tools, technology, rest, exercise, and compensation (to put a roof over your head and food on the table)
- *Psychological safety needs*, which include security, trust, predictability, organizational integrity, and freedom to fail and to speak up
- *Belonging needs*, which include community, friendship, respect, empowerment, and the opportunity to contribute and to be authentic

- *Need for meaning*, which includes purpose, progress to goals, access to information, challenging work, ownership, and opportunities for learning and creativity.

Physical needs are what economists call *hygiene factors*—there is a base value for just staying alive, but very few of us live at that level. Instead, the need is based on what we get used to. So, it might feel like a reward to get a bonus at first, but we quickly normalize to that compensation level, so the next bonus is perceived as just meeting a basic need, and not getting a bonus feels like deprivation. As a safety professional, you are meeting several important physical needs, but as a leader, your greatest responsibility is to fulfill psychological safety, belonging, and meaning needs. Addressing the latter is also your greatest opportunity for motivating your team and improving performance.

TYPE OF NEED	EMOTIONS	EXAMPLE NEEDS
Physical	Sadness Dissatisfaction	A safe and comfortable work environment, tools, technology, rest, exercise, and compensation.
Psychological Safety	Fear Insecurity	Security, trust, predictability, organizational integrity, and freedom to fail and to speak-up.
Belonging	Loneliness Defiance	Community, friendship, respect, empowerment, and the opportunity to contribute and to be authentic.
Meaning	Confusion Detachment	Purpose, progress to goals, access to information, challenging work, ownership, and opportunities for learning and creativity.

A simple practice for developing empathetic concern is simply to explore what a person or group needs when you detect a painful emotion. There's a reason sales professionals call customer needs *pain points*—people don't always know what they need, but they know where they hurt. When you scan a meeting for the vibe or notice someone's mood, if you detect dissatisfaction, dejection, confusion, insecurity, frustration, anger, fear, or sadness, inquire about needs. Let's consider the pre-job brief for that delayed process that has created frustration for you and the team. You might say, "I know it's been frustrating getting to this point. What do you all need going forward to alleviate that frustration and feel like we are making meaningful progress?" That's it. Just ask people what hurts and what they need.

I won't get into conflict management here. There are plenty of excellent books describing various effective techniques. I'll just say that the practices I have described here are the basis for difficult and destructive emotional reactions, like that which plagues effective incident investigations—blame. Yes, *it fixes nothing*, but it is a normal emotional defense against fear, surprise, anger, and shame. Let's take the common example of an expert making a mistake. Your coyotes howl: "How could such a smart person be so stupid?" You pause and reflect on how you feel: "I feel scared. If this person could do that, how out of control might this operation be?" You take a breath and apply a constructive lens: "I had no idea this could even happen—I'm humbled by this incident. I am grateful the controls worked and that the consequences weren't more serious. If this is scary for me, I can feel compassion for the terror felt by the people who were there." Now others get into the fray and angrily demand you hold this person accountable. You recognize their emotions: "When I heard about the incident, I was scared that others might make this same mistake, so I can understand why you would feel angry." Pause to give them time to express their anger. Help reframe the situation for them: "I'm grateful that I now know this mistake can happen, even with an expert, just when we are now employing less experienced people. This gives us an opportunity to improve the process before new people start doing it." Now explore their needs: "What do you need to feel more secure that we can control for this type of incident in the future?" At this point, you will have managed the emotions of the situation to put yourself in a good position for problem-solving and creating more safety capacity in your organizational, operational, and psychological systems.

Emotional Resiliency Reflection Questions

1. Do you ever engage in behaviors you wish you wouldn't, like staying late at work when you committed to going home on time, doing a task yourself that you should have delegated, or even just eating dessert when you aren't hungry? Without engaging in any rationalizations for that behavior (just accept it, it happened), try to think about what you were doing or thinking right before that behavior and how it made you feel. If you can't recall, try to write down your feelings as soon as you find yourself doing it again. What might you do to create a pause between your emotion and the behavior?

2. Think about a leader who earned your trust. Even if you didn't know them well, did they seem to empathize with you? If so, in what ways did they demonstrate their understanding of your perspective? How did they show that they cared about your feelings or recognized your needs?

3. Identify an action or attitude someone recently did that you did not approve of. Even though you don't agree with the behavior, do you think it's possible to empathize with the person who did it? Can

you recognize their perspective, even if you don't share it? Can you acknowledge their feelings even if you don't feel the same? Can you identify what needs they were trying to fulfill with the behavior, even if they didn't effectively meet those needs?

4. Think about an aspiration you once had that you didn't achieve. How might achieving that aim have met your needs? (In other words, why did you want to do it?) Thinking back on that time, what other needs did achieving that aspiration compete with? For example, if you wanted to get a certification, might the time needed to study for the test compete with your need to spend time with your family? Now imagine that you are negotiating a compromise between those competing needs. How would you have resolved the competing interests? Can you think of an example at work where you can do a similar negotiation between the competing needs of individuals, groups, or functions?

CHAPTER 8: BUILD SAFETY CAPACITY

There are no born leaders, just people who practice leadership regularly.

The purpose of the six leadership practices I have shared with you in the previous pages is to build the capacity in your organization, its operations, and your people to recover and learn from failure. Failure is simply the occurrence of the unexpected, unintended, or unwanted—there doesn't need to be a bad consequence for something to be a failure. Building safety capacity in your organizational, operational, and psychological systems is what reduces the negative consequences of failure and reaps the benefits of it.

Leadership is an important safety system that influences all levels of the organization

Leadership shapes the meaning and purpose of work by setting goals and defining what success means, by orchestrating how people and groups work together and make decisions, by facilitating communication and relationships, and by distinguishing roles and responsibilities. To create a capacity for safety, safety leaders must integrate learning and resiliency into all these activities.

This book is a how-to guide for doing just that. But what I have outlined here aren't solutions; they are practices. Capacity must be continuously built and maintained, because it must continuously respond to changing conditions, emerging hazards, and other unknowns. I would like to leave you with a blueprint for integrating these practices into the leadership of your team, project, function, or organization:

Shape a shared purpose

The first practice for building safety capacity involves identifying a shared purpose with which people and groups can align, and regularly communicating that purpose. This builds safety capacity by helping leaders recognize and resolve the disagreements and tensions that are creating misalignment between strategic objectives and operating conditions, cultural drivers, and/or worker incentives. The practice is simple: make shaping a shared purpose part of the formation of any team, project, initiative, collaboration, partnership, etc. Revisit that purpose, continue to clarify it, and continue to communicate it. Always have this question at the ready, "Okay, before we go on, let's remind ourselves, what's our purpose here?"

Cultivate networks of relationships

Organizations are social systems built on networks of relationships. Safety capacity relies on the strength, vitality, and diversity of those relationships because information, insight, resources, and the ability to learn and adapt flows along those networks. The leadership practice of identifying and cultivating the relationships that are important to strategic perspective, operational support, and learning might be the most challenging practice described in these pages, but it is certainly of the highest imperative. Safety is a team effort. Because the relationships in social systems are vast and complex, it's important to approach networking intentionally. Identify those who can supply you and your team with information, resources, and subject matter expertise, as well as those who have the power to make decisions that impact safety. Develop a plan to build and maintain the most important relationships, and include your team members in both the planning and the relationship cultivation and management. I'm not advocating for transactional relationships—this is an activity of enhancing the meaning of work and strengthening shared purpose.

Foster openness and curiosity

If the black line was reality and we could be certain that workers would never be confronted with emerging hazards, shifting conditions, and ambiguous expectations, then learning, and the resiliency that results from it, would not be necessary. I hope the cases presented in this book have demonstrated conclusively that learning is fundamental to safe operations. To learn, we must be open to the unexpected, and curious about failure. The leadership practice of fostering open and curious mindsets in yourself and in your team is twofold: first, continuously scan for change, and second, regularly look for gaps between the expected, the desired, and the reality. Both these activities are easy, if you shape a culture that values learning over being right.

Drive critical thinking

So many of the cases described in this book demonstrate the importance of critical thinking. The practice of disrupting bias, questioning assumptions, broadening perspectives, and generating multiple solutions to problems helps leaders both build safety capacity and avoid unintentionally undermining it with short-sighted decisions. A step many leaders skip in the rush to find a solution to a pressing issue is to robustly define the problem. When considering safety capacity, it's important to take into consideration the interpersonal dynamics around the problem because it is usually these dynamics that either drive or hinder change. I shared with you in chapter 5 the CHIP model to use as a template for assessing the consequences, habits, identity, and power dynamics affecting your issue. If you use the CHIP model to better define your problem and integrate other critical thinking techniques into your regular problem-solving practices, you will avoid many of the cognitive traps and decision pitfalls uncovered in incident investigations.

Experiment

In a VUCA (volatile, uncertain, complex, and ambiguous) environment, if you aren't experimenting, you are gambling. Little erodes safety capacity more than the unknown. Experimentation is a learning technique for creating knowledge and increasing certainty, and there is no need for it to be expensive, time-consuming, or complicated. This leadership practice begins with just stating your hypothesis. When we decide or act, we have a hypothesis; we just rarely take the time to examine it. The discipline of an experimental approach helps us evaluate the effectiveness of our actions, learn if our assumptions are correct, and build a better understanding of the conditions we are working in. All of this builds safety capacity by increasing our knowledge of what can fail and improving our methods for prevention and recovery.

Develop emotional resiliency

I would have begun this book with this chapter because emotional resiliency is a crucial leadership skill for leaders, especially safety leaders. Leadership literature is full of studies on the importance of emotional intelligence and other emotional management skills to leadership and organizational performance. Emotional skills certainly underlie the other five leadership practices described in this book, yet I believe the most compelling benefit to safety capacity is the power it gives leaders to recover emotionally from failure so they can learn. This is a power you can impart to your teams, many times just by modeling it. Emotional skills are developed through observing, practicing, and experiencing. The techniques I described for you in chapter 7 are very simple, but they aren't terribly comfortable. It may take some willpower to continue practicing them, but I promise the rewards will be immense, not only for safety capacity but for your own capacity to learn.

Finally, I recommend you take some time to contemplate and revisit the reflection questions I added at the end of each chapter. My decades of leadership development facilitation have taught me that it mostly depends on individual reflection and self-assessment. Even if you read this book in one afternoon, I hope you take your time answering the reflection questions and practicing the techniques shared within these pages designed to help you build safety capacity in your organization and operations.

ABOUT THE AUTHOR

DR. MARTHA ACOSTA is an internationally regarded speaker, facilitator, and expert in Human and Organizational Learning who helps organizations with high-risk operations navigate the complexity of human systems in their operations. A consultant and trainer since the mid-1990s, Martha has helped countless leaders manage volatility, uncertainty, and ambiguity. She is also a senior moderator for Harvard Business Publishing's corporate learning division. Before joining Harvard, Martha designed and delivered leadership classes for technology companies, including Cisco Systems, Intel, and Apple. She also led the Human Performance Improvement Team for the nuclear facilities at Los Alamos National Laboratory (LANL), where she helped develop a national safety initiative for the Department of Energy and won LANL's Director's Achievement Award. Todd Conklin called her the "Godmother of HOP" on his Preaccident Investigation podcast. Martha began her career in Silicon Valley helping fast-growing technology companies build the sales and support capacity needed to commercialize their innovative solutions. Later, she led the design and delivery of global leadership programs for a subsidiary of News International in the United Kingdom.

Martha is a passionate community volunteer and holds leadership positions on non-profit boards. She chairs committees on the Board of Visitors and Governors of St. John's College in Annapolis, Maryland, and Santa Fe, New Mexico. She is also an officer on the board of the Los Alamos National Laboratory Foundation, which supports underserved students, teachers, and schools in Northern New Mexico. She previously sat on the Board of Homewise, a non-profit affordable housing developer and mortgage bank, and on the alumni boards of two of her alma maters.

Martha earned a doctorate in Human and Organizational Learning from the George Washington University in Washington, DC, and both a Master of Business Administration and Master of Arts from Southern Methodist University in Dallas, Texas. She also completed a graduate credential in training systems development from San Francisco State University. She earned her BA from St. John's College in Annapolis, Maryland.

Made in the USA
Coppell, TX
16 January 2026